Absolute
LOVE

Absolute
LOVE

R. I. Willroth

WestBow
PRESS
A DIVISION OF THOMAS NELSON

WestBow Press books may be ordered through booksellers or by contacting:

WestBow Press
A Division of Thomas Nelson
1663 Liberty Drive
Bloomington, IN 47403
www.westbowpress.com
1-(866) 928-1240

Because of the dynamic nature of the Internet, any web addresses or links contained in this book may have changed since publication and may no longer be valid. The views expressed in this work are solely those of the author and do not necessarily reflect the views of the publisher, and the publisher hereby disclaims any responsibility for them.

Certain stock imagery © Thinkstock.
Any people depicted in stock imagery provided by Thinkstock are models, and such images are being used for illustrative purposes only.

Scripture quotations are from The Holy Bible, English Standard Version® (ESV®), copyright © 2001 by Crossway, a publishing ministry of Good News Publishers. Used by permission. All rights reserved.

ISBN: 978-1-4497-1838-1 (e)
ISBN: 978-1-4497-1839-8 (sc)
ISBN: 978-1-4497-1840-4 (hc)

Library of Congress Control Number: 2011930146

Printed in the United States of America

WestBow Press rev. date: 6/2/2011

Contents

Introduction

I have often heard that politics and religion should be two topics you want to avoid. Perhaps if one had little conviction about any matter, the avoidance of these subjects could work out. I have also heard from my childhood if you don't have anything constructive to say, then don't say anything at all. Perhaps this is the reason we avoid topics we are very passionate about—because we haven't looked for ways to engage those we disagree with constructively.

Can a Muslim, a Christian, and a Jew find a constructive beginning point for dialogue? Can an avowed atheist or an agnostic put down some of their personal and intellectual walls to engage in constructive discussion about absolutes? Is there some absolute beginning point from which everyone can start to agree and then learn from the others?

I am writing this book for those who would like to begin that discussion. I acknowledge that I have biases; I would like those biases if they have no basis for existing to be exposed. I also believe that there is one connecting absolute that we'll agree upon. The absolute is that love is universal; love is an absolute among human beings. We all want to be loved; we all feel the need for love, and we all yearn to have another person whom we can share love with.

At the outset, I will state that all religions believe that their God is sovereign or absolute. Yet all uniquely declare that God wants to be loved (or they might say *worshipped*), and that they believe God loves them. This book is about what, or to be more exact *who*, love *is*. Love exists and the topic of this book is where love comes from, why love is an absolute, who this absolute love is, what this absolute love looks like, and what the characteristics of love are. I hope it to be relevant to everyone. I know not everyone will agree with me.

My point is that love exists and that love is an absolute. Yet not everyone will agree on how to define love or where love comes from. In this study, I come to the conclusion that love is an entity, one entity, a unity of substance, purpose, and power. Love is a personal being that is ultimate power and absolute personhood. All else is relative to love, created by love, sustained by love, defined by love, and ultimately judge by love.

Love is not sentimentality, not weak capitulation to others, not passive acceptance of all things, and certainly not sexual intercourse. Love is humility, belief, trust, acceptance, confidence, gratitude, compassion, freedom, stewardship, servanthood, loyalty, purity, justice, rest, and determination. Love is the overflowing character of the only absolute in the universe. It flows throughout the One who is love and establishes everything.

Humility is the characteristic of believing that gives us the ability to admit our needs, weaknesses, and limitations so that we can submit to the power of God in our life and receive our strength from Him and through others. It is not powerlessness; it knows where the power comes from. Humility is the beginning of faith that love works in us as we look outside of ourselves to I AM. Humility involves being able to give to others but also to receive from others as we keep our eyes fixed on I AM and thereby become more like Him in love. The key characteristic of humility is mercifulness. The loss of humility brings about rebelliousness.

Belief is an overwhelming sense of hope based on understanding of past actions and in the fulfillment of future promises that gives encouragement so that we can be enthusiastic and self-stretching, in order that we might grow through developing (God-given) potential. The key characteristic of belief is hopefulness. The loss of belief brings about despair.

Trust is the characteristic outgrowth of believing that gives us the ability to be open and share who we are and what we have been given so that we can be catalysts in the development of openness and candor in others. The key characteristic of trust is openness. The loss of trust brings about suspiciousness.

Acceptance is the characteristic outgrowth of believing that gives us the ability to forgive ourselves and others so that healing and understanding can take place. The key characteristic of acceptance is forgiveness. The loss of acceptance brings about a judgmental nature.

Confidence is the characteristic outgrowth of believing that gives us assurance of our being accepted and gives us the ability to look past self-promotion to the promotion of others so that their confidence is built up. The key characteristic of confidence is assuredness or certainty. The loss of confidence brings about inconsistency.

Gratitude is the characteristic outgrowth of believing that gives us the ability to look at all good things as gifts from God and causes us to give in return so the gifts can be shared by all. The key characteristic of gratitude is thankfulness. The loss of gratitude brings about an expecting nature: ungratefulness.

Compassion is the characteristic outgrowth of believing that gives us the ability to be gracious (giving undeserved favor) and merciful (not demanding retribution) so that we might live in a way that will be most beneficial to ourselves and others and glorify God. The key characteristic of compassion is graciousness. The loss of compassion brings about degradation, the using of others.

Freedom is the characteristic outgrowth of believing that gives us the ability to set aside personal desires and postpone pleasure (i.e., physical and emotional gratification), in order that we are liberated to find complete satisfaction in God and be separated from enslaving entanglements. The key characteristic of freedom is purposefulness. The loss of freedom brings about insatiability, the inability to be satisfied.

Stewardship is the characteristic of believing that gives us the ability to be inter-connected with each other in a truly loving manner. We do not lose any integral parts of ourselves or disintegrate into another person, yet we value and need each other's gifts and uniqueness for the full use and completion of our own giftedness. The key characteristic of stewardship is carefulness. The loss of stewardship brings about codependence, an inability to be helpful.

Servanthood is the characteristic of believing that gives us the ability to worship in everything that we do by looking to God to fill us and overflow through us into the lives of others for thoughtful attentiveness to God's desires for them. The key characteristic of servanthood is submissiveness or interdependence. The loss of servanthood brings about an uncaring attitude, inattentiveness.

Loyalty is the characteristic outgrowth of believing that gives us the ability to remain true or faithful to I AM, ourselves, and others so that we are not pushed or led along by demands other than God's. The key characteristic of loyalty is faithfulness. The loss of loyalty brings about inconsistency.

Purity is the characteristic outgrowth of believing that gives us the ability to be unmixed in our allegiance toward God so that we won't be driven by any other purpose than to love, glorify, and enjoy God to the ultimate benefit, enjoyment, and fulfillment of ourselves and others. The key characteristic of purity is objectiveness (integrity, congruence). The loss of purity brings about confusion.

Justice is the characteristic outgrowth of believing that gives us the ability to act rightly on behalf of God so that despots (those who want to control, oppress, and use others for personal gain) are not allowed to triumph and the defenseless are defended. The key characteristic of justice is righteousness. The loss of justice brings about either apathy or being overbearing (despotism).

Rest is the characteristic of believing that gives us the ability to see past obstacles to our own well-being and the well-being of others so that we can peacefully work to overcome those obstacles and overthrow those who are setting them up. The key characteristic of rest is peacefulness. The loss of rest brings about anxiety, panic.

Determination is the characteristic of believing that gives us the ability to persist until that which has been started is completed. The key characteristic of determination is steadfastness, completion. The loss of determination brings about an inability to follow through, indecision.

These characteristics are not exhaustive of who absolute love is, but they are a beginning point. Absolute love is inexhaustible.

CHAPTER ONE

Absolutes

Absolutes. Might there be an absolute something or someone? There is a scary possibility—that one person or group of people could proclaim their idea as absolute. The thought of someone else placing his or her idea of absolute upon me, as an individual, brings up all kinds of thoughts of rebellion and rejection.

My daughter's elementary school staff and the school administrators must believe that absolutes exist, at least for good elementary students. Without asking about religious or personal preferences, the school impressed upon all of the children the "absolute truths" of the "six pillars of character."

Through a search of the Web, I found this reference to the Character Counts program: "The CHARACTER COUNTS! approach to character education doesn't exclude anyone. That's why we base our programs and materials on six ethical values that everyone can agree on—values that are not political, religious, or culturally biased ..."[1]

The universally desired "absolute" character traits are as follows:[2]

> Trustworthiness
> Be honest • Don't deceive, cheat, or steal • Be reliable—
> do what you say you'll do • Have the courage to do the

right thing • Build a good reputation • Be loyal—stand
by your family, friends, and country

Respect

Treat others with respect; follow the Golden Rule •
Be tolerant and accepting of differences • Use good
manners, not bad language • Be considerate of the
feelings of others • Don't threaten, hit, or hurt anyone •
Deal peacefully with anger, insults, and disagreements

Responsibility

Do what you are supposed to do • Plan ahead • Persevere:
keep on trying! • Always do your best • Use self-control
• Be self-disciplined • Think before you act—consider the
consequences • Be accountable for your words, actions,
and attitudes • Set a good example for others

Fairness

Play by the rules • Take turns and share • Be open-
minded; listen to others • Don't take advantage of others
• Don't blame others carelessly • Treat all people fairly

Caring

Be kind • Be compassionate and show you care • Express
gratitude • Forgive others • Help people in need

Citizenship

Do your share to make your school and community better
• Cooperate • Get involved in community affairs • Stay
informed; vote • Be a good neighbor • Obey laws and rules
• Respect authority • Protect the environment • Volunteer

These seem to me to be very good character traits; according to the
people who defined these traits, they are absolute. "They are values that

everyone can agree on." The originators claim, "These values are not politically, religious or culturally biased."[3]

To clarify this discussion of absolute values, consider several dictionary definitions of absolute.

Noun	1.	absolute—something that is conceived or that exists independently and not in relation to other things; something that does not depend on anything else and is beyond human control; something that is not relative.
Adj.	1.	absolute—perfect or complete or pure.
	2.	absolute—complete and without restriction or qualification.[4]

Religious concepts of God do not often resemble these definitions as they carry social and political baggage specific to a region or country. Formalized religious organizations, in order to unite, set up doctrines and rules not seen as absolute, even within the greater body of religious believers. The history of Christianity, for instance, includes an early split between Constantinople and Rome, and then a later split between Rome and the Protestant Reformation.

I grew up in a small Protestant church group started, in this country, by immigrants to the United States escaping from persecution under the state-run Lutheran Church for their beliefs in a specific doctrine of Christian baptism. In Sweden, after the establishment of a Lutheran state church, people who later made a public testament to their faith by submitting to adult baptism by immersion were sought out and drowned.

This book does not aim to establish some religious doctrine or rule of action. I do intend to hold up two truths about God I believe are held as absolute by all the "people of the Book"—Jews, Christians, and Muslims. God is absolute; all truth is relative if not established by the God who is absolute. I hope that dialogue and openness can characterize discussions about absolutes. I believe everyone can affirm that if an absolute exists, this absolute is what all people would call God. When people believe God exists, they must believe that God is the absolute. Each person and every thought receives absolute truth in relationship to God. Likewise, apart from direct confirmation from God by revelation, all things exist relative to partiality to incomplete and possibly flawed or perverted versions of the truth. All three religious "people of the Book"—historically Jews, Christians, and Muslims—claim their roots and their God to be the God of Abraham, a Middle Eastern Bedouin who lived some four thousand years ago.

I know what you're thinking. Where is this going? Are you crazy? These religions do nothing but fight with each other! Do you remember or have you even heard of all the history of fighting and killing?

If you will walk through this study with me, whether you are a Jew, a Muslim, an agnostic, an atheist, a Christian, or a holder of some other religion or worldview, an inner revolution may take place. You may find that you *do not know all the answers.* You may find a benefit in a deeper conversation about these issues. You may find that repentance in some form may be in order. Could a change of viewpoint be helpful? A word from Dr. John White might be an aid at this point:

> I do not believe, however, that all inner revolutions are equally positive or healthy. My experience has shown me that repentance is positive only to the extent that it involves aligning oneself, with the way the universe is made. Reality is not subjective; there is a moral structure to the universe. The essence of positive and lasting change is aligning ourselves with that structure.[5]

I ask you to walk with me on a journey away from political, social, and religious rhetoric and toward a search for absolutes and, ultimately, toward an understanding of what it means to love absolutely.

Dietrich Bonhoeffer writes about the ethical dilemma of deciding upon the good. His work has helped me to think through the idea of absolute love.

Whoever wishes to take up the problem of a Christian ethic must be confronted at once with a demand which is quite without parallel. He must from the outset discard as irrelevant the two questions which alone impel him to concern himself with the problem of ethics, "How can I be good?" and "How can I do good?," and instead of these he must ask the utterly and totally different question, "What is the will of God?" This requirement is so immensely far-reaching because it presupposes a decision with regard to the ultimate reality; it presupposes a decision of faith. If the ethical problem presents itself essentially in the form of inquiries about one's own being good and doing good, this means that it has already been decided that it is the self and the world which are ultimate reality. The aim of all ethical reflection is, then, that I myself shall be good and that the world shall become good through my action. But the problem of ethics at once assumes a new aspect if it becomes apparent that these realities, myself and the world, themselves lie embedded in a quite different ultimate reality, namely, the reality of God, the Creator, Reconciler and Redeemer. What is of ultimate importance is now no longer that I should become good, or that the condition of the world should be made better by my action, but that the reality of God should show itself everywhere to be the ultimate reality. Where there is faith in God as the ultimate reality, all concern with ethics will have as its starting-point that God shows Himself to be good, even if this involves the risk that I myself and the world are not good but thoroughly bad. All things appear distorted if they are not seen and recognized in God. All so-called data, all laws and standards are mere abstractions so long as there is no belief in God as the ultimate reality. But when we say that God is ultimate reality, this is not an idea, through which the world as we have it is to be sublimated. It is not the religious rounding-off of a profane conception of the universe. It is the acceptance in faith of God's showing forth of Himself, the acceptance of His revelation. If God were merely a religious idea there would be nothing to prevent us from discerning, behind this allegedly "ultimate" reality, a still more final reality, the twilight of the gods and the death of the gods. The claim of this ultimate reality is satisfied only in so far as it is revelation, that is to say, the self-witness of the living God. When this is so, the relation to this reality is not merely a gradual advance towards the discovery of ever more profound realities; it is the crucial turning-point in the apprehension of reality as a whole. The ultimate reality now shows itself to be at the same time the initial reality, the first and the last, alpha and omega. Any perception or apprehension of things or laws without Him is now abstraction, detachment from the origin and goal. Any inquiry about one's own goodness, or the goodness of the world, is now impossible unless inquiry has first been made about the goodness of God. For without God what meaning could there be in a goodness of man and a goodness of the world ...

Good is now no longer a valuation of what is, a valuation, for example, of my own being, my outlook or my actions, or of some condition or state in the world. It is no longer a predicate that is assigned to something which is in itself in being. Good is the real itself. It is not the real in the abstract, the real which is detached from the reality of God, but the real which possesses reality only in God. There is no good without the real, for the good is not a general formula, and the real is impossible without the good. The wish to be good consists solely in the longing for what is real in God. A desire to be good for its own sake, as an end in itself, so to speak, or as a vocation in life, falls victim to the irony of unreality. The genuine striving for good now becomes the self-assertiveness of the prig. Good is not in itself an independent theme for life; if it were so it would be the craziest kind of quixotry. Only if we share in reality can we share in good.[6]

I thought these words from Bonhoeffer may help others see my thought process regarding two often quoted but misguided maxims concerning truth. Each of these thoughts, I believe, conveys some degree of reality but not *ultimate* (absolute) reality. Often we hear academics saying, "All truth is relative," especially secular academics. More frequently, of late, we hear evangelical Christian academics saying, "All truth is God's truth." At first my reaction is to stand with the latter statement and reject the former. Yet, having contemplated the ramifications of each statement, I am more inclined to slightly change the first statement and reject the second out of hand. Instead, I think we should say, "Some truth is relative," and "Only absolute revealed truth is God's truth."

One thing that brings me to think *This is the way we should think about truth* is Jesus' confrontation with a man who asked, "Good teacher, what shall I do to inherit eternal life?" Jesus replied, "Why do you call me good? No one is good except God alone."

John Piper writes, "God never had a beginning! 'I am' has sent me to you. And one who never had a beginning, but always was and is and will be, defines all things. Whether we want him to be there or not, he is there. We do not negotiate what we want for reality. God defines reality. When we come into existence we stand before a God who made us and owns us. We have absolutely no choice in this matter. We do not choose to be. And when we are, we do not choose that God be. No ranting and raving, no sophisticated doubt or skepticism, has any effect on the existence of God. He simply and absolutely is. 'Tell them 'I am' has sent you.'"

If we don't like it, we can change our mind, for our joy, or we can suppress this truth, to our destruction. But one thing remains absolutely unassailed: God is. He was there before we came. He will be there when we are gone. Therefore what matters above all things is this God. I cannot escape the simple and obvious truth that God must be the main thing. Life has to do with God because every atom and every emotion and every soul of every angelic, demonic, and human being belongs to God, who absolutely is. He created all that is, he sustains everything in being, and he directs the course of all events, because "from him and through him and to him are all things, to him be glory (in our ministries!) forever" (Romans 11:36).[7]

M. Scott Peck has written about this ethical dilemma by saying, "To be ethical is, at the very least, to be 'humanistic,' which by definition means having the attitude that people are precious ... The problem with secular humanism is that it says nothing about why human beings are precious, nor why they should be treated accordingly. Consequently, secular humanism, being unrooted in any kind of theology, is often a fair weather phenomenon. That is why I define civil behavior not simply as 'ethical' but specifically as 'ethical in submission to a higher power.' For if, as I said light, truth, and love are all synonyms of a sort for God, and if we are truly submitted to these things, our behavior will be godly even though we may not think of ourselves as religious." [8]

A third contemplation is Einstein's theory of relativity, where at least part of this theory sorts out for us how matter distorts the space/time continuum. Through that, we have been able to discover how the earth's gravitational pull alters the use of energy, allowing us to discover, among many other important applications, how to travel outside our earth's atmosphere. The sciences tell us that empirical data is altered by both the limitations (constraints) that we put upon experimentation and the presuppositions that guide the processes of experimentation. We must therefore, if we are honest, conclude that through empirical sciences we know relative truth. That is, truth that is only true to the limitations that we have placed upon that truth in our finite understanding.

What has been said should not lead us to believe that nature (or truth revealed by nature) is unreal. $E=MC^2$ is a verifiable formula or equation. Nature is governed by laws that are unbreakable, because they are derived from ultimate reality. But what has been said does mean, unless we see these realities as pointing back to the ultimate reality, the meaning of these verifiable truths will be subject to relativism. "For since the creation of the world His invisible attributes, His eternal power and divine nature, have been clearly seen, being understood through what has been made, so that they are without excuse." Romans 1:20 According to Einstein's theory, there is no observable absolute motion, only relative motion. There must be something ultimate to which our understanding of truth is relative, or measured against. This is a probable explanation to why educational institutions from the Judeo-Christian world have developed scientific theories of practical impact and economical value to a much greater degree than the rest of the world.

So, if we accept that we are finite (limited) beings, we will acknowledge that what we do know from experience is not absolutely true or absolute reality. Absolute reality must be revealed by the absolute, or else it is distorted. This is why it is absolute folly for man to try to gain understanding apart from a living relationship with God. Distortion, perversion, and absolute error are the ramifications of saying "all truth is God's truth."

On the other hand, the importance of humility in handling revealed truth, and "speaking the truth in love" is a great caution for us to hold on to if we feel we know what God has revealed as truth. In our finitude and limited understanding ("now we know in part"—"we see through a glass dimly"), we can be far from the mark of the application God wants us to convey. Our understanding of situations is always limited (relative) to not knowing all of the circumstance. This includes all of our understanding of God, though it is reality revealed in His Word (The Bible); our understanding is limited in perspective. An example is the caution of James to "being quick to hear, slow to speak and slow to anger; for the anger of man does not achieve the righteousness of God." Our anger, even if justified, is limited to our perspective. "All our righteousness is as filthy rags." Therefore anger in us produces, more often than not, immoral or unrighteous results. Yet God can be angry and bring about righteousness. "He made Him who knew no sin, to be made sin on

our behalf, so that in Him we might become the righteousness of God."
2 Cor. 5:21 This is why judgment is so heinous to Jesus and why blame
and shaming of others is improper and unhelpful in changing behavior
in others.

So, let us be compassionate toward one another and acknowledge
that, in so far as it goes, some truth is relative. If we are open and honest
and unafraid to face this fact, then perhaps we can dialogue with them
about truth in a way that does not alienate. On the other hand, let us be
careful about what truth we assign to God and, in all humility, let Him
define what that truth is.

J. I. Packer says, "We are children, and therefore victims, of reaction—
negative stances of recoil blinding us to the value in the things we reject.
Human reaction never results in God's righteousness; it is not discerning
enough ...

"I am talking about what sociologists call *cultural prejudice.* I am saying
we all suffer from it, most of all those of us who think we don't, and that
as a result, we are constantly missing things that are there for us in the
Bible. We are ourselves part of the problem of understanding because of
the way that tradition and reaction have conditioned us. When, therefore,
we ask God to give us understanding, we should be asking him to keep us
not only from mistakes about meaning of texts but also from culturally
determined blind spots. We cannot hope in this world to lose our blinkers
entirely; we shall always be men and women of our time, nurtured by
our cultural milieu and also narrowed by it. That is the inescapable
human condition. But we can at least be aware of the problem, and try
to surmount it as far as possible."[9]

As Albert Einstein cautioned, 'we should take care not to make the
intellect our god. It has, of course, powerful muscles, but no personality.
It cannot lead, it can only serve."[10]

When I was in junior high school, our teacher had two boys in our
class stage a fight at the beginning of class. This, though a very realistic
conflict, was all planned ahead of time, though none of us knew that.
The fight was broken up by the teacher and the two boys were sent out
of the room, supposedly to the principal's office, and the teacher came

back in asking for any viewpoints as to how the fight might have started. Of course, you can already guess that there were several different versions and differences of opinion as to who was at fault. The same thing happens in regard to reporting of accidents, mediating disputes, getting differing opinions from physicians, and educators arguing dogmatically on either side of the nature/nurture debate. Those who trust in empirical sciences as absolutes should take a look at the variances between separate dating of fossilized material using carbon 14 methodology. Likewise, students of psychology need to weigh the differences between successes of behavioral theorists and psycho-dynamic theorists. This is not to say that truth, absolute truth, is incompatible with natural truth, but truth learned naturally (truth revealed by nature) must come under investigation by revealed truth. Also, truth learned naturally can at times, merely be relative truth.

As M. Scott Peck explains, "Science, therefore, is an activity submitted to a higher power (except of course, in those instances when the ego of scientists get in the way of their search for truth). Since God is the epitome of our higher power—God is light, God is love, God is truth—anything that seeks these values is holy. Thus, while it cannot answer all questions, science, in its proper place, is a very holy activity." [11]

Returning to Bonhoeffer's point, the question of what is good is not a question that can be answered very well from a finite perspective. For instance, we know that it is not good to, out of love for a family member who is alcoholic (or any addictive behavior we might name), compensate for the inabilities that are brought on by that addiction. On the other hand, compensation for others' inabilities is the essence of spirit giftedness in the body of Christ. This type of interdependency is very good. Therefore, when we are told to do good and bless those who hate and persecute us for being devoted to Jesus, it does not mean we become helpful to them in doing so. We must balance the good of blessing with the call to provide justice to the defenseless and the truth that love provides for discipline. "Those whom the LORD loves He reproves and disciplines." So, to ask what is good in a relative sense can be very unhelpful. As Bonhoeffer says, we need to ask "What is the will of God?" [12]

CHAPTER TWO

Love IS

If you call yourself a believer, or aren't sure what you believe, let's agree at the outset to this: loving your families, your husbands and wives, your children, your brothers and sisters, and your neighbors is a much better way to live than being in turmoil and constantly fighting. As Stephen Carter has written, "But if we have no time to listen with love and respect to those who disagree with us, then we have no time for awe in God's creation, and thus no time for lives of civility."[1]

I know there are differences. My two sisters and my brother, though we grew up together, are definitely different, and we all live in different parts of the United States. We don't always agree on everything, but I know they would stand up for me and care for me in need. It really helps that we have a long history together and know what the others have been through in life. We understand where each other is coming from. How can we be more effectively involved in learning from and loving one another? From Steven Covey we hear, "Seek first to understand then to be understood."[2]

If your are set in your mind that you don't believe faith has any benefit but to start war and strife, I think you can still agree that loving one another or at least getting along is a better way to live than ignoring or scoffing at others who have an absolute frame of reference. At least you can acknowledge that all the questions about our existence have not been answered yet. People are still seeking and it might not hurt to at least know why they are so passionate. Perhaps you will welcome a doctor's advice. "Love is intimately related with health. This is not a sentimental exaggeration. One survey of ten thousand men with heart disease found a 50 percent reduction in frequency of chest pain (angina) in men who perceived their wives as supportive and loving," says Larry Dossey, MD, in his book, *Healing Words.*[3] Dr. Dossey also goes on to document the value of belief in God. He says, "Over two dozen studies demonstrate the health promoting effects of simply attending church or synagogue on a regular basis." The doctor also cites work by Jeffrey S. Levin, PhD, where he says; "Levin has uncovered over 250 empirical studies in which spiritual or religious practices have been statistically associated with particular health outcomes ... Positive effects for both morbidity and mortality have been found for cardiovascular disease, hypertension, stroke, nearly every type of cancer, colitis and enteritis."[4]

I am aware that there are important differences between Jews, Christians, and Muslims. There are also wide gaps between people of faith and atheists. In fact, there are differences among various groups within all three faiths. I grew up in a small Baptist denomination and a joke went around that if you put three Baptists in a room together, the only thing they could agree on was that there should be three Baptist churches in town. However, if you have come with me this far, let's together see if we can find some common ground—maybe even some absolutes?

The journey toward knowing who God is starts with God revealing His name to us. Jews, Christians, and Muslims are all people of a revealed God, an absolute creator. In the Tanakh, the writings of Jesus' followers (who were Jewish by birth and faith), and the Koran, I believe we can come to at least six points of agreement among believers in God as to the nature of God.

- God is absolutely self-existent. God was, is, and forever shall be uncreated and unending.
- God is absolutely sovereign.

- God is creator and sustainer of life, beginning and end. Life exists and continues to exist because God persists in allowing life to exist.
- God is absolutely personal, in other words God is a unique personal being. There is no other being like God. God is wholly other that created beings.
- God is absolutely self-revealing. We only know God as He has revealed Himself to us. We are finite; God is eternal and beyond our discovery unless God allows us glimpses into eternity.
- God is a relational God. If God has chosen to reveal Himself, then God is relational in the sense that He reaches out to relate to us.
- God is absolutely love. To explain what I mean that God is absolutely love is the reason for this book. Love is the character of God, but it is a differently defined love than we think of or exhibit ourselves. I know this is difficult to comprehend, but it is what is revealed. (I probably will need to do some more convincing on this point.)

The truth is there is often so much cultural or political history that mitigates against loving others from different countries, political reference points, religious contexts and intellectual points of view. It is very difficult to let go of what we know and reach out to what is unknown. We cannot imagine things as being different from our present frame of reference and rebuild our paradigms in other directions is seemingly impossible.

G. K. Chesterton says, "Nobody can imagine how nothing could turn into something. Nobody can get an inch nearer to it by explaining how something could turn into something else. It is really far more logical to start by saying 'In the beginning God created heaven and earth' even if you mean 'In the beginning some unthinkable power began some unthinkable process.' For God is by its nature a name of mystery, and nobody ever supposed that man could imagine how a world was created any more than He could create one."[5]

All three "religions of the book" claim their God to be the God of Abraham. Our journey to finding the absolute begins in the Tanakh (the Jewish Holy Book) consisting of three parts: the law, the prophets, and the writings). Christians have also claimed the Tanakh as the part of their Bible usually called the Old Testament. This shouldn't be very surprising—Jesus of Nazareth was Jewish and followed Jewish customs, such as going to the Jewish temple to celebrate Passover at age twelve. All of the writers of the Christian New Testament grew up following Jewish customs and they filled their writings with quotes from the Tanakh.

Abram, later called Abraham, was a Bedouin who lived in the Middle East over four thousand years ago. Judaism, Christianity, and Islam all trace their roots back to this area and the man named Abraham. In the Tanakh it is recorded.

Genesis 11:31–12:4: "Terah took Abram his son and Lot the son of Haran, his grandson, and Sarai his daughter-in-law, his son Abram's wife, and they went forth together from Ur of the Chaldeans to go into the land of Canaan, but when they came to Haran, they settled there ... Now the LORD said to Abram, 'Go from your country and your kindred and your father's house to the land that I will show you. And I will make of you a great nation, and I will bless you and make your name great, so that you will be a blessing. I will bless those who bless you, and him who dishonors you I will curse, and in you all the families of the earth shall be blessed.' So Abram went, as the LORD had told him, and Lot went with him. Abram was seventy-five years old when he departed from Haran."

The word LORD in this passage is in Hebrew יהוה or YHWH ,.

The word *YHWH* is never spoken out loud in strict Jewish traditions. "The LORD" is always said out loud when this personal name for God is encountered in the reading of the Tanakh. It is considered irreverent to say the name aloud. YHWH in the root is a form of the personal pronoun I. YHWH is usually rendered "I AM" or "I AM that I AM" The name speaks to God's absoluteness, self-existence, eternality, sovereignty, personal existence, and self-revealing character.

These characteristics are also found within the Koran. "And your god is One God; there is none who has the right to be worshipped but

He, the Most Beneficent, the Most Merciful" (Quran 2:163). "God! There is no god but Him, the Living, the Self-Sufficient. He is not subject to drowsiness or sleep. Everything in the heavens and the earth belongs to Him. Who can intercede with Him except by His permission? He knows what is before them and what is behind them but they cannot grasp any of His knowledge save what He wills. His Footstool encompasses the heavens and the earth and their preservation does not tire Him. He is the Most High, the Magnificent" (Quran 2:255).

That God is absolute, a frame of reference by God and derived only from God, can be agreed upon by Christians, Muslims, and Jews. If you are presently, by which I mean *temporarily*, atheistic or agnostic, you surely will not agree that God is absolute. You may agree, though, that persons exist and that existence seeks some permanence, some absoluteness, either within or outside of oneself. According to an often repeated philosophical axiom from philosopher Rene Descartes, "I think therefore I am." If you will permit ... I will, for myself, drop the necessarily ambiguous God as the subject of this journey and call the One who I am referring to as "I AM" or "the One who is," sometimes simply as "absolute love" for that is my deduction. I do this out of reverence for "I AM" and to use a reference that might carry less baggage for everyone involved. I AM carries with it the connotation of absoluteness. But wait: my assertion is that *love is.*

That love exists possibly poses a greater barrier to atheistic thinking than the fact that horrible atrocities are committed in the name of some people's god. The atrocities committed by people often pose a barrier to the notion that "I AM" exists. As C. S. Lewis writes in, *The Problem of Pain,* "Until the evil man finds evil unmistakably present in his existence, in the form of pain, he is enclosed in the illusion. Once pain has roused him, he knows that he is in some way or other 'up against' the real universe: either he rebels (with the possibility of clearer issue and deeper repentance at some later stage) or else makes some attempt at an adjustment, which, if pursued will lead him to religion." [6]

Religion though is most often a way of appeasing or gaining God's favor, but love or I AM is not looking for anything that could gain favor; we have nothing to give except love in return. I AM as self existence is in need of nothing. I AM's relationship with us is an overflow of love because *love is*. We don't need to appease I AM. There is no way that we could. As Dr John Piper writes in the book *Desiring God*, "God has no deficiencies that I might be required to supply. He is complete in himself. He is overflowing with happiness in the fellowship of the Trinity. The upshot of this is that God is a mountain spring, not a watering trough. A mountain spring is self-replenishing. It constantly overflows and supplies others. But a watering trough needs to be filled with a pump or bucket brigade. So if you want to glorify the worth of the watering rough you work hard to keep it full and useful. But if you want to glorify the worth of the spring you do it by getting down on your hands and knees and drinking to your heart's satisfaction, until you have the refreshment and strength to go back down in the valley and tell the people what you've found. You do not glorify a mountain spring by dutifully hauling water up the path from the river below and dumping it in the spring. What we have seen is God is like a mountain spring, not a watering trough. And since God is the way God is, we are not surprised to learn from Scripture—and our faith is strengthened to hold fast—that the way to please God is to come to him to get and not to give, to drink and not to water. He is most glorified in us when we are most satisfied in him."[7]

To believe in this God is a giant step on the way to personal growth, because it will involve a significant amount of loss—loss of self and surely loss of things that we have held as dear to us. It will cost the loss of things we now love to find absolute love.

Robert Greenleaf in his book on leadership writes, "No one can judge, from where one now stands, how difficult the next step along the road of spiritual growth will be. Those of good works, the upright moral citizens, and the pillars in the church may find the next step of staggering proportions. Their seeming opposites—the unsuccessful, the misfit, the unlovely, and the rejected—may take the next step with ease. We cannot assume with assurance that we are relatively advantaged or disadvantaged for any stage of the inward journey.

"To be on the journey one must have an attitude toward loss and being lost, a view of oneself in which powerful symbols like burned, dissolved, broken off—however painful their impact is seen to be—do not appear as senseless or destructive. Rather the losses they suggest are seen as opening the way for new creative acts, for the receiving of priceless gifts. Loss, every loss one's mind can conceive of, creates a vacuum into which will come (if allowed) something new and fresh and beautiful, something unforeseen—and the greatest of these is love. The source of this attitude toward loss and being lost is faith: faith in the validity of one's own inward experience; faith in the wisdom of the great events of one's history, events in which one's potential for nobility has been tested and refined; faith in doubt, in inquiry, and in the rebirth of wisdom; faith in the possibility of achieving a measure of sainthood on this earth from which flow concerns and responsibility and a sense of rightness in all things. By these means mortals are raised above the possibility of hurt. They will suffer, but they will not be hurt because each loss grants them the opportunity to be greater than before. Loss, by itself, is not tragic. What is tragic is the failure to grasp the opportunity which loss presents."[8]

Look with me at the earliest of revelations of I AM with Adam and Eve. God sets up a paradise a garden that Adam and Eve have neither need nor wants but to enjoy the relationship they have with each other, the world around them and with I AM. I AM sets up one single matter of trust with them not to eat of the tree of the knowledge of good and evil. Outside of loving and trusting relationship with one another and outside of loving and trusting relationship with I AM they were breaking faith.

Can you imagine giving someone your everything, all he needs or could want, being totally open and loving toward him, yet in desire to keep him from harmful effects you ask him to stay away from a person you know may corrupt and harm him? I will let you imagine that person's characteristics yourself. You come home at night and the person you love is nowhere to be found. You call and call and the loved one doesn't answer. Finally you find him or her hiding in a corner, disheveled and shaken. The person cannot look at you. You know that trust has been broken. Your loved one no longer wants your love and protection. He or she is not sorry for the breach of trust; he or she excuses it and holds up very good reasons for doing what he or she did. He or she is filled with defiant blame even amid the shame of being exposed. He or she doesn't care that it showed great disrespect and ultimately a lack of love toward you. What would you do?

I AM covered them with clothes and promised to make things right. I AM showed that He cared even though they had betrayed trust. However broken trust has brought broken relationship and separation. Separation has caused severe consequences and because I AM is love, the giver and sustainer of life, death will come and begin with a real inability to love in the same way as I AM is love.

Fast-forward through Genesis and part of Exodus. I AM has shown to overflow with love to people though people continue to be hateful and dangerous toward each other. I AM has seen the back-breaking slavery of the descendants of Abraham. I AM seeks always to release from bondage and tyranny to replace people in a loving environment/community. The descendants of Abraham are freed from the deadly rule and religion of the Egyptians. The community of refugees is brought to a mountain where Moses, their leader and the representative of I AM, is to go up to the mountain to receive instructions from I AM.

On the mountain, I AM instructs Moses and writes on two tablets of stone the summary of those instructions. There are basically two parts of the instructions given. The first is *love I AM!* and the second is *love each other!* Because of the separation from I AM, the instructions had to be more detailed. The connection to love is still broken and the ability to be in the image of I AM is perverted.

Moses in receiving the revelation from I AM is gone a long time, and, while he is gone, the people who have just been led out of bondage and tyranny turn back to the gods and the religion of the land they have been rescued from. Instead of a loving relationship, they again turn to the bondage of religion.

Moses realizes that, without the very presence of God, any attempt at establishing the community in love is impossible. Moses says, "Now therefore, if I have found favor in your sight, please show me now your ways, that I may know you in order to find favor in your sight. Consider too that this nation is your people. And he said, 'My presence will go with you, and I will give you rest.' And he said to him, 'If your presence will not go with me, do not bring us up from here. For how shall it be known that I have found favor in your sight, I and your people? Is it not in your going with us, so that we are distinct, I and your people, from every other people on the face of the earth?' And the LORD said to Moses, 'This very thing that you have spoken I will do, for you have found favor in my sight, and I know you by name.' Moses said, 'Please show me your glory.' And he said, 'I will make all my goodness pass before you and will proclaim before you my name 'The LORD.' And I will be gracious to whom I will be gracious, and will show mercy on whom I will show mercy'" (Exodus 33:13–19).

Here is the moment of I AM telling Moses about His character. What is the absolute nature of God? Exodus 34:5–7: "The LORD descended in the cloud and stood with him there, and proclaimed the name of the LORD. The LORD passed before him and proclaimed, 'The LORD, the LORD, a God merciful and gracious, slow to anger, and abounding in steadfast love and faithfulness, keeping steadfast love for thousands, forgiving iniquity and transgression and sin, but will by no means clear the guilty ...'"

Do you notice the description? In my own words: "I AM, I AM merciful, gracious, I don't get angry very easily, I overflow with steadfast love and faithfulness, I continue forever to keep overflowing with love for thousands, I continually forgive your wrong doing, immorality, and your just plain blowing it. Still I will make sure justice is done."

The essence of I AM is overflowing *hesed* (loving kindness, steadfast love, absolute love). In Hebrew it is a word that is translated and used as loyalty, kindness, mercy, beauty, devotion, faithfulness, and goodness. The connotation is so full of meaning it is almost indefinable to us. The sense is of an overflowing, unbounded love that spills over from the inner being of I AM.

This conclusion of who God is resonates with Hebrew followers of Jesus. John, who is the last survivor of those who were the initial followers and friends, writes (1 John 4:16–19) "So we have come to know and to believe the love that God has for us. God is love, and whoever abides in love abides in God, and God abides in him. By this is love perfected with us, so that we may have confidence for the day of judgment, because as he is so also are we in this world. There is no fear in love, but perfect love casts out fear. For fear has to do with punishment, and whoever fears has not been perfected in love. We love because he first loved us."

John says, "God is love." The word that is translated *love* here is from the ancient Greek language: *agape*. Love in the sense of agape is unexpected love, a kind of love that stops you in amazement, a love that goes beyond understanding that flows undeserved and unbounded from the giver. It is sacrificial, absolute love. This love is beyond natural; it gives from the essence of the giver and not because of anything derived from the recipient. I AM is love. Love overflows from the essence of I AM. It is sometimes defined as unconditional; I believe that is a misunderstanding. This love may be said to be sacrificial love, but not selfless love, not unconditional love. It is absolute love flowing out from within the self of God. It is absolute love flowing out from God. The conditions come from the absoluteness of I AM. It is definitely sacrificial love, but it is not unconditional. Absoluteness is unalterable and I AM must maintain absoluteness or in turn love will be diminished. As I AM says to Moses in Exodus 33:19, "And he said, 'I will make all my goodness pass before you and will proclaim before you my name 'The LORD.' And I will be gracious to whom I will be gracious, and will show mercy on whom I will show mercy.'" Absoluteness, not arbitrariness. It is not arbitrary because it flows from the absolute character of love. I AM reserves the justice of his overflowing love by maintaining the absoluteness of his character: "I will by no means clear the guilty." This is not unconditionality, it is demanding. The guilty are those who continue to deny love IS, who will not accept love, and who will not cherish love.

This very idea was concisely stated in believers in the past by the statement, "The chief end of man is to glorify God and enjoy Him forever." Dr. John Piper recently, in his book *Desiring God*, has restated that phrase by saying, "The chief end of man is to glorify God by enjoying Him forever."[9] This is what I AM intended for mankind in the beginning.

In the Quran there are ninety among the ninety-nine names of God, the most famous and most frequent are "the Compassionate" (*al-rahman*) and "the Merciful" (*al-rahim*). These names portray the meaning of being beneficent, gracious, caring, having tender affection for or in relationship to Allah, the most merciful in essence.

That love *is*, or that God is love, is the conclusion of the Tanakh, the Quran, and the New Testament. All three look for a Savior, a redeemer. The Tanakh does not name this Messiah except with the title "The Son of Man," a title that Yeshua, the carpenter's son, clearly used for Himself. The Quran clearly names him Isa Al-Masih. This same Yeshua was born in Bethlehem, Judea. Yeshua (in Hebrew, the language of the Tanakh), Isa (Aramaic language of the Quran) and Jesus (Greek language of the New Testament) name the same person who lived in Nazareth with his parents over two thousand years ago. This conclusion is *no pie in the sky, head in the sand* declaration. I realize there are significant differences between the proponents of each faith. If you can walk a bit farther with me, laying aside the differences for now, hold on to the fact that love *is*.

Hesed (loving/kindness, steadfast love, fidelity, mercy, goodness, compassion, kindness) the Hebrew word used in the Tanakh that describes indescribable unimaginable love is used in the following passages.

Genesis 19:19, 20:13, 21:23, 24:12, 24:14, 24:27, 24:49, 32:10, 39:21, 40:14, 47:29, Exodus 15:13, 20:6, 34:6, 34:7, Leviticus 20:17, Numbers 14:18, 14:19, Deuteronomy 5:10, 7:9, 7:12, Joshua 2:12, 2:14, Judges 1:24, 8:35, Ruth 1:8, 2:20, 3:10, 1 Samuel 15:6, 20:8, 20:14, 20:15, 2 Samuel 2:5, 2:6, 3:8, 7:15, 9:1, 9:3, 9:7, 10:2, 15:20, 16:17, 22:51 ,1 Kings 2:7, 3:6, 4:10, 8:23, 20:31, 1 Chronicles 16:34, 16:41, 17:13, 19:2, 2 Chronicles 1:8, 5:13, 6:14, 6:42, 7:3, 7:6, 20:21, 24:22, 32:32, 35:26, Ezra 3:11, 7:28, 9:9, Nehemiah 1:5, 9:17, 9:32, 13:14, 13:22, Esther 2:9, 2:17, Job 6:14, 10:12, 37:13, Psalm 5:7, 6:4, 13:5, 17:7, 18:50, 21:7, 23:6, 25:6, 25:7, 25:10, 26:3, 31:7, 31:16, 31:21, 32:10, 33:5, 33:18, 33:22, 36:5, 36:7, 36:10, 40:10, 40:11, 42:8, 44:26, 48:9, 51:1, 52:1, 52:8, 57:3, 57:10, 59:10, 59:16, 59:17, 61:7, 62:12, 63:3, 66:20, 69:13, 69:16, 77:8, 85:7, 85:10, 86:5, 86:13, 86:15, 88:11, 89:1,

89:2, 89:14, 89:24, 89:28, 89:33, 89:49, 90:14, 92:2, 94:18, 98:3, 100:5, 101:1, 103:4, 103:8, 103:11, 103:17, 106:1, 106:7, 106:45, 107:1, 107:8, 107:15, 107:21, 107:31, 107:43, 108:4, 109:12, 109:16, 109:21, 109:26, 115:1, 117:2, 118:1, 118:2, 118:3, 118:4, 118:29, 119:41, 119:64, 119:76, 119:88, 119:124, 119:149, 119:159, 130:7, 136:1, 136:2, 136:3, 136:4 136:5, 136:6, 136:7, 136:8, 136:9, 136:10, 136:11, 136:12, 136:13, 136:14, 136:15, 136:16, 136:17, 136:18, 136:19, 136:20, 136:21, 136:22, 136:23, 136:24, 136:25, 136:26, 138:2, 138:8, 141:5, 143:8, 143:12, 144:2, 145:8, 147:11, Proverbs 3:3, 11:17, 14:22, 14:34, 16:6, 19:22, 20:6, 20:28, 21:21, 31:26, Isaiah 16:5, 40:6, 54:8, 54:10, 55:3, 57:1, 63:7, Jeremiah 2:2, 9:24, 16:5, 31:3, 32:18, 33:11, Lamentations 3:22, 3:32, Daniel 1:9 9:4, Hosea 2:19, 4:1, 6:4, 6:6, 10:12, 12:6, Joel 2:13, Jonah 2:8, 4:2, Micah 6:8, 7:18, 7:20, Zechariah 7:9.

Agape (love) the Greek word used in the New Testament (Injeel) that describes indescribable unimaginable love is used in the following passages.

Matthew 24:12, Luke 11:42, John 5:42, 13:35, 15:9, 15:10, 15:12, 15:13, 17:26, Romans 5:5, 5:8, 8:35, 8:39, 12:9, 13:10, 14:15, 15:30, 1 Corinthians 4:21, 8:1, 13:1, 13:2, 13:3, 13:4, 13:8, 13:13, 14:1, 16:14, 16:24, 2 Corinthians 2:4, 2:8, 5:14, 6:6, 8:7, 8:8, 8:24, 13:11, 13:14, Galatians 5:6, 5:13, 5:22, Ephesians 1:4, 1:15, 2:4, 3:17, 3:19, 4:2, 4:15, 4:16, 5:2, 6:23, Phil 1:9, 1:17, 2:1, 2:2, Colossians 1:4, 1:8, 1:13, 2:2, 3:14, 1 Thessalonians 3:6, 5:8, 5:13, 2 Thessalonians 1:3, 2:10, 3:5, 1 Timothy 1:5, 1:14, 2:15, 4:12, 6:11, 2 Timothy 1:7, 1:13, 2:22, 3:10, Titus 2:2, Phile 1:5, 1:7, 1:9, Hebrews 6:10, 10:24, 1 Peter 4:8, 5:14, 2 Peter 1:7, 1 John 2:5, 2:15, 3:1, 3:16, 3:17, 4:7, 4:8, 4:9, 4:10, 4:12, 4:16, 4:17, 4:18, 5:3, 2 John 1:3, 1:6, 3 John 1:6, Jude 1:2, 1:12, 1:21, Revelation 2:4, 2:19 Agapao Matthew 5:43, 5:44, 5:46, 6:24, 19:19, 22:37, 22:39, Mark 10:21, 12:30, 12:31, 12:33, Luke 6:27, 6:32, 6:35, 7:5, 7:42, 7:47, 10:27, 11:43, 16:13, John 3:16, 3:19, 3:35, 8:42, 10:17, 11:5, 12:43, 13:1, 13:23, 13:34, 14:15, 14:21, 14:23, 14:24, 14:28, 14:31, 15:9, 15:12, 15:17, 17:23, 17:24, 17:26, 19:26, 21:7, 21:15, 21:16, 21:20, Romans 8:28, 8:37, 9:13, 9:25, 13:8 13:9, 1 Corinthians 2:9,

8:3, 2 Corinthians 9:7, 11:11, 12:15, Galatians 2:20, 5:14, Ephesians 1:6, 2:4, 5:25, 5:28, 5:33, 6:24, Colossians 3:12, 3:19, 1 Thessalonians 1:3, 1:4, 3:12, 4:9, 2 Thessalonians 2:13, 2:16, 2 Timothy 4:8, 4:10, Hebrews 1:9, 12:6, James 1:12, 2:5, 2:8, 1 Peter 1:8, 1:22, 2:17, 3:10, 2 Peter 2:15, 1 John 2:10, 2:15, 3:10, 3:11, 3:14, 3:18, 3:23, 4:7, 4:8, 4:10, 4:11, 4:12, 4:19, 4:20, 4:21, 5:1, 5:2, 2 John 1:1, 1:5, 3 John 1:1, Revelation 1:5, 3:9, 12:11, 20:9.

End Notes

1. Carter, Stephen L. *Civility*. Basic Books. New York, NY, 1998, page 140.
2. Covey, Steven. *The Seven Habits of Highly Effective People*. Fireside Books, Simon and Schuster, Inc., New York, NY, Habit # 5 pages 235-260.
3. Dossey, Larry MD. *Healing Words: The Power of Prayer and the Practice of Medicine*. HarperCollins, New York, NY, 1993, page 109.
4. IBID, pages 251-252.
5. Chesterton, G. K. *The Everlasting Man*. Ignatius Press, San Francisco, CA, first published by The Royal Literature Fund, 1925, reprinted 1993, 2008, pages 24-25.
6. Lewis, C. S. *The Problem of Pain*. McMillan Publishing, New York, NY, 1962, twenty-first printing 1978, page 95.
7. Piper, Dr. John. *The Pleasures of God; Meditations on God's Delight in Being God*. Multnomah Publishers, Inc., Sisters, OR, 1991, pages 215-216.
8. Greenleaf, Robert K. *Servant Leadership*. Paulist Press, New York, NY, 1977, page 327.
9. Piper, Dr. John. *Desiring God; Confessions of a Christian Hedonist*. Multnomah Publishers, Inc. Sisters, OR, 1986, page 14.

CHAPTER THREE

Fear, Faith, and love

I AM seems a vague a name for the one who is love, for God. I often have a difficult time with uncertainty and not knowing. It is the history of man to try to manipulate and control. As this is true, it demonstrates a deep level of mistrust and a lack of love. The very nature of man in response to questioning by the serpent was to misconstrue and go along with the implied mistrust of the questioning. Genesis 3:1: "Now the serpent was more crafty than any other beast of the field that the LORD God had made. He said to the woman, 'Did God actually say, 'You shall not eat of any tree in the garden?''" Genesis 3:4: "But the serpent said to the woman, 'You will not surely die.'"

Fear takes away the ability to be in the presence of absolute love and, because I AM is beyond us, a completely other being, we separate ourselves. In fear we try to make I AM more manageable; we try to make I AM into our image and likeness. This is the way we want to worship a god; we want a god we can fully understand and somewhat control, not the eternal, all-powerful, all-knowing creator but a created likeness so we make images and idols. We fashion a god, or gods, that have some power, in as much as it serves our thinking and supposed needs. Yet these little imaginings of ours are not absolutes. They cannot really help us get past our fear. So we establish rituals and rules because they give us some sense of control. Yet we are still afraid of unknowns and fear keeps us from absolute love. Fear ultimately brings death. David Viscott, MD, says, "No one can deal with fear of the unknown, for it is fear without limitation. It contaminates your judgment and paralyzes you ... When you live in fear, you bring upon yourself the very losses you dread most."[1]

What happens when we become separated from I AM? We start blaming, we feel shame, we want to hide, and we don't want to be exposed. Genesis 3:10–13: "And he said, 'I heard the sound of you in the garden, and I was afraid, because I was naked, and I hid myself.' The man said, 'The woman whom you gave to be with me, she gave me fruit of the tree, and I ate.' Then the LORD God said to the woman, 'What is this that you have done?' The woman said, 'The serpent deceived me, and I ate.'"

Trust is broken; the ability to walk with I AM is forfeited. Love requires relationship and the building blocks of a loving relationship consist of at the least fifteen qualities of faith that establish the basis for continuing in relationship. These fifteen qualities of faith, that come from abiding in love, are humility, belief, trust, acceptance, confidence, gratitude, compassion, freedom, stewardship, servanthood, loyalty, purity, justice, rest, and determination.

These qualities flow from and through I AM; absolute love, they come from Him as a result of walking with Him and being in His presence. Genesis 5:24: "Enoch walked with God, and he was not, for God took him." This mysterious passage gives hint to the relationship that I AM desires: a simple walking alongside is all. This is what was happening in the first instance of I AM's relationship with mankind. They thought (and we think) that I AM might be withholding something really desirable from us, so we look for fulfillment outside of I AM. Instead of receivers we become takers, even hoarders. Instead of satisfaction we find that our needs are insatiable and we die. Genesis 3:17–19: "And to Adam he said, 'Because you have listened to the voice of your wife and have eaten of the tree of which I commanded you, 'You shall not eat of it,' cursed is the ground because of you; in pain you shall eat of it all the days of your life; thorns and thistles it shall bring forth for you; and you shall eat the plants of the field. By the sweat of your face you shall eat bread, till you return to the ground, for out of it you were taken; for you are dust, and to dust you shall return.'"

Dr. John White says, "All of us have an insatiable craving to be loved. And we have a deep down fear that we won't be." Love is essential to all higher life forms. The higher the life form, the more necessary love becomes to physical survival. Without love we begin, quite literally, to die. For this reason all of us harbor a terrible fear of rejection. They may be buried deep in our unconscious minds. Yet subtly and powerfully, these feelings influence our behavior and distort our view of life around us. The deep and insatiable need for love and the consequent fear of rejection lie at the root of our difficulty in changing."[2]

Not only have we become takers without ever finding a way to satisfy our desires, not only are we dying, but we also kill one another. Genesis 4:3–12: "In the course of time Cain brought to the LORD an offering of the fruit of the ground. And Abel also brought of the firstborn of his flock and of their fat portions. And the LORD had regard for Abel and his offering, but for Cain and his offering he had no regard. So Cain was very angry, and his face fell. The LORD said to Cain, 'Why are you angry, and why has your face fallen? If you do well, will you not be accepted? And if you do not do well, sin is crouching at the door. Its desire is for you, but you must rule over it.' Cain spoke to Abel his brother. And when they were in the field, Cain rose up against his brother Abel and killed him. Then the LORD said to Cain, 'Where is Abel your brother?' He said, 'I do not know; am I my brother's keeper?' And the LORD said, 'What have you done? The voice of your brother's blood is crying to me from the ground. And now you are cursed from the ground, which has opened its mouth to receive your brother's blood from your hand. When you work the ground, it shall no longer yield to you its strength. You shall be a fugitive and a wanderer on the earth.'"

Even in the ways we try to please I AM, we fail because we are not connected to the love that flows from I AM. In our need we become more fearful, and that fear produces rebellion, despair, suspicion, a judgmental nature, uncertainty, insatiable desire, ungratefulness, degradation of others, codependences', uncaring attitudes, unreliability, bullying, the inability to follow through, anxiety, and a sense of being confused.

We carry a deep inability within ourselves to not be able to hold out absolute love apart from the connection to I AM. So we live in fear. We fear our weakness, we fear our frailty, and we fear being rejected by others. Yes, we even fear being killed when we are all dying. Dr. John White, a psychiatrist, calls all of what I have been describing an even harsher reality. He calls the result of this fear in us evil. In his book *Changing on the Inside*, Dr. White says, "Beyond the philosophical debates, however, we must deal with human actions and decisions. Here on this basic level, evil is hard to deny and even harder to accept. Evil vaunts its proud hatred in religion, in politics, in every aspect of life. We have only to think of racial hatred and violence, or the abuse and abandonment of children, or the blind greed of corporations to know that evil must be fought wherever it appears. Evil on this planet typically has to do with 'man's inhumanity to man.' This reality reveals itself in cruelty, exploitation of the weak, racism, violence and sexual exploitation in families. It manifests itself primarily in the disruption of the relationships we have with one another as human beings. Evil cannot be tolerated. But can it be overcome? That question rests at the heart of the issue of change ... How explain it? Evil is part of the reality of who we are. It exists in us all because we—the entire human race—have chosen to run our lives our own way. If we believe we have evil under control, then we have never seriously tried to get rid of it." [3]

I, deep down, say, "I am not evil." Oh, sure, at times I might callously think, *Why should I burden myself with other people's pain or problems?* But I have never really hurt anyone. I most of the time have no trouble with my self-esteem or thinking well of myself. I feel occasionally bad that some people have not liked me. I, more seldom than I should, feel bad that I don't lose the weight that my doctor tells me to lose. I have never stolen from another person or killed anyone. Then I remember how, when a young boy, some friends and I stole some cigarettes and smoked them out behind the bushes. I remember that I turned pale green and was sicker than any flu I have had. I remember my parents not making a very big issue with the episode because I was so sick. I also remember several times becoming annoyed and angry enough to kill. When my younger brother would goad me, I would chase him around yelling "I'm going to kill you." Then there was that time ... Oh, my. And then that other time! As I recall those memories, my failures and inconsistencies become innumerable. Yet I continue to think of myself as not so bad.

M. Scott Peck, MD, explains, "We need moments when we realize that we do not have it all together and that we are not perfect ... So there is a difference between insisting that we always feel good about ourselves(which is narcissistic and synonymous with constantly preserving our self-esteem) " and " ... the further we proceed in diminishing our narcissism, our self-centeredness and sense of self-importance, the more we discover ourselves becoming less fearful of death but also less fearful of life. And this is the basis for learning to be more loving. No longer burdened by the need to constantly protect and defend ourselves, we are able to lift our eyes off ourselves and truly recognize others. And we begin to experience a sustained, underlying sense of happiness that we have never experienced before as we become progressively more self-forgetful and hence more able to remember God ..."[4]

While fear causes us to be unloving toward others, it also can have devastating physical effects, especially if the fear is incessant or prolonged. The following is an excerpt from a public blog by Dr. Anthony DeMarco on the physiological effects fear can have on a person. "The first noticeable change is an increase in perspiration as well as heart and respiratory rates. This physical reaction is due to the activation of a small, walnut-sized structure in the forebrain called the amygdala. This structure, in turn, then stimulates the hypothalamus to produce CRH, or corticotrophin-releasing hormone. This hormone, then, triggers the production of adrenocorticotropic hormone, known as ACTH, in the pituitary gland, a small, oval gland at the base of the brain. Finally, this signal travels to the adrenal gland, sitting just above the kidney, which produces cortisol, causing an increase in glucose production to provide additional fuel for the muscles and brain to deal with the stress. This complex series of direct communications between the hypothalamus, pituitary gland, and adrenal gland is known as the hypothalamic-pituitary-adrenal, or HPA, axis, a vital and major part of the neuroendocrine system that controls the reaction to stress, amonsgt other body processes. Clearly, the simple physical responses to fear are the product of a chain of biological events."[5]

Dr. Demarco goes on to explain some of the physical changes caused by a sense of fear: "When one is confronted by a perceived threat, there are many more physical responses that are less evident, such as: pupil dilation; increased muscle tone; decreased blood flow to the skin, intestine and kidneys; and bowel and bladder emptying."[6]

When fear is prolonged and incessant, it can become anxiety and cause anxiety attacks as Dr. DeMarco explains: "Often, manifestations called panic attacks can develop. These episodes carry many of the same symptoms as heart attacks, and are often misinterpreted as such. Anxiety can last for as long as the stressor is evident, and it has been linked, through various studies, to a myriad of health issues, such as arthritis, migraines, allergies, and thyroid disease."[7]

The prolonged effect of this fear and anxiety can have devastating effects on us physically, as Dr. DeMarco explains: "Most commonly, continuous anxiety has been linked to gastrointestinal problems, such as peptic ulcers. While a mechanism tying these disorders together has yet to be discovered, studies have shown a remarkable correlation of people who have experienced both generalized anxiety disorder, or GAD, and stomach ulcers. Chronic anxiety has also been linked to cardiovascular disease." [8]

The fear we carry from being unloving and uncaring is a difficult burden to carry. Most of the time we deny and ignore the fears we have. Sometimes we turn to activities, or substances, that alter our physical and emotional responses, to mask, dampen, or deaden the fear. Every recovery program that I know of begins with an acknowledgement that we have a problem and are in trouble. In most recovery programs, we need to admit that we are powerless to overcome the problem and we must admit the need for help from a higher power, a power outside ourselves.

To remember and be reminded, to believe that I AM is love, is the most life-changing of things to have as a gift in life. To be able to draw near in relationship with love is a life altering phenomenon. The presence of I AM changes us. In fact we were fashioned to be like the person we are most close to in relationship. Relational connections change us. Children take on characteristics of their parents; peers take on characteristics of their companions; and married partners take on characteristics of their mates. If it is a very good partnership, a mutually giving, loving partnership will help each of them to take on the best parts of the other. The partners become a better entity together than they would be apart. In the book *Primal Leadership*, the authors say, "Research in intensive care units has shown that the comforting presence of another person not only lowers the patient's blood pressure, but also slows the secretion of fatty acids that block arteries. More dramatically, whereas three or more incidents of intense stress within a year (say, serious financial trouble, being fired, or divorce) triple the death rate in socially isolated idle-aged men, they have no impact whatsoever on the death rate of men who cultivate many close relationships ... one person transmits signals that can alter hormone levels, cardiovascular function, sleep rhythms and even immune function inside the body of another. That's how couples who are in love are able to trigger in one another's brains surges of oxytocin, which creates a pleasant, affectionate feeling. But in all aspects of social life, not just love relationships, our physiologies intermingle, our emotions automatically shifting into the register of the person we're with. The open-loop design of the limbic system means other people can change our very physiology- and so our emotions." [9]

No wonder I AM said if you eat of the fruit forbidden by me you will die. To be separated from the giver of live, from love, mankind would no longer have access to the tree of life. To break the trust of I AM and our relationship with life and love would cause a process of fear and death to begin. "If you want to go it on your own deciding what you know as the difference between good and evil you must go apart from me," says I AM. "You are subject to your limitedness as a creature, I am absolute love and I cannot remain loving in the midst of allowing evil." We do not recognize how evil unbelief really is; it destroys our lives. Yet love does not leave us in this spiral of death. However, I AM continues to come back time and time and time again in rescue missions. What is meant by saying God is love is not what is often thought. C. S. Lewis talks about our misconceptions of the love of God: "Of course, what these people mean when they say that God is love is often something quite different: they really mean 'love is God.' They really mean that our feelings of love, however and wherever they arise, and whatever they arise, and whatever results they produce, are to be treated with great respect. Perhaps they are; but that is something quite different from what Christians mean by the statement 'God is love.' They believe that the living, dynamic activity of love has been going on in God for ever and has created everything else."[10]

Let's look deeper into what *God is love* means. In the declaration of the glory of I AM to Moses, the phrase "visiting the iniquity of the fathers on the children and the children's children, to the third and the fourth generation." it is most often thought this is a declaration of continued judgment on and on to future generations. I do not agree. In fact, the Hebrew word here *paqad* can mean "visit either for good or bad intention." It can be translated as "deliver or oversee." In the time of this text, it was most often used of visiting a village that had been plundered by marauders in order to see to the needs of the survivors. Spiros Zodhiates, in his Lexicon of Old Testament words, says of paqad, "It's true meaning is an action taken on the part of God which produces a beneficial result for His people. (See Ruth 1:6, 1 Samuel 2:21; Jeremiah 29:10.)"[11]

When I AM gives Moses a glimpse of His glory by declaring (Exodus 34:6-10) "The LORD passed before him and proclaimed, 'The LORD, the LORD, a God merciful and gracious, slow to anger, and abounding in steadfast love and faithfulness, keeping steadfast love for thousands, forgiving iniquity and transgression and sin, but who will by no means clear the guilty, visiting the iniquity of the fathers on the children and the children's children, to the third and the fourth generation. And Moses quickly bowed his head toward the earth and worshiped. And he said, 'If now I have found favor in your sight, O Lord, please let the Lord go in the midst of us, for it is a stiff-necked people, and pardon our iniquity and our sin, and take us for your inheritance. And he said, 'Behold, I am making a covenant. Before all your people I will do marvels, such as have not been created in all the earth or in any nation. And all the people among whom you are shall see the work of the LORD, for it is an awesome thing that I will do with you.'"

It is clear that Moses believed I AM's presence in the midst of the people was the prerequisite for their survival. It was also clear that I AM was not going to give up on these people even though they had broken the integrity of the relationship. He certainly wasn't going to continue to visit them to their destruction. I AM was going to continue to visit them for their ultimate benefit.

This is the struggle all throughout history recorded for the people of the book: to have faith in the One who is love. To accept that I AM is the source, and sustainer of a life of love is our continued struggle. To pursue a renewed relationship with love is the way to life and will result in the removal of fear. I will let one of the closest followers of Jesus say it more eloquently: 1 John 4:16–21: "So we have come to know and to believe the love that God has for us. God is love, and whoever abides in love abides in God, and God abides in him. By this is love perfected with us, so that we may have confidence for the day of judgment, because as he is so also are we in this world. There is no fear in love, but perfect love casts out fear. For fear has to do with punishment, and whoever fears has not been perfected in love. We love because he first loved us. If anyone says, "I love God," and hates his brother, he is a liar; for he who does not love his brother whom he has seen cannot love God whom he has not seen. And this commandment we have from him: whoever loves God must also love his brother."

For this reason, other writers of the Bible can write in regard to whether to eat foods that were offered to idols. Romans 14:23: "But whoever has doubts is condemned if he eats, because the eating is not from faith. For whatever does not proceed from faith is sin."

Sin and evil are not essentially the actions of our life. Ultimate evil is the rejection of faith that I AM is love. To stop believing or to have a heart full of doubt about I AM breaks connection, for I AM cannot become something He is not or He ceases to be. The great King David in the Tanakh says this in Psalm 51:4–17: "Against you, you only, have I sinned and done what is evil in your sight, so that you may be justified in your words and blameless in your judgment. Behold, I was brought forth in iniquity, and in sin did my mother conceive me. Behold, you delight in truth in the inward being, and you teach me wisdom in the secret heart. Purge me with hyssop, and I shall be clean; wash me, and I shall be whiter than snow. Let me hear joy and gladness; let the bones that you have broken rejoice. Hide your face from my sins, and blot out all my iniquities. Create in me a clean heart, O God, and renew a right spirit within me. Cast me not away from your presence, and take not your Holy Spirit from me. Restore to me the joy of your salvation, and uphold me with a willing spirit. Then I will teach transgressors your ways, and sinners will return to you. Deliver me from bloodguiltiness, O God, O God of my salvation, and my tongue will sing aloud of your righteousness. O Lord, open my lips, and my mouth will declare your praise. For you will not delight in sacrifice, or I would give it; you will not be pleased with a burnt offering. The sacrifices of God are a broken spirit; a broken and contrite heart, O God, you will not despise."

I AM wants us to return to relationship with Him in faith. It is this loss of connection, brokenness of relationship, that causes death and the fear of death, so we live in fear.

It is my hope to see a picture of I AM in this book that will help build faith, hope, and love in us. 1 Corinthians 13:13: "So now faith, hope, and love abide, these three; but the greatest of these is love." If you are Muslim, or a follower of Judaism, I pray that references from the Bible will not keep you from continuing on the journey. We all need to begin to learn more of faith and love. If you are an atheist, I ask that you continue to seek for places that might allow you to have faith. Faith begins in the seeking heart. Jeremiah 29:11–14: "For I know the plans I have for you, declares the LORD, plans for welfare and not for evil, to give you a future and a hope. Then you will call upon me and come and pray to me, and I will hear you. You will seek me and find me, when you seek me with all your heart. I will be found by you, declares the LORD, and I will restore your fortunes ..."

Fear is a characteristic of uncertainty, which is rooted in the suppression of truth and accompanied by guilt and shame. This *fear* begins with an inability to believe or not having someone to believe in, that is, not having someone who is ultimately good and loving to rely upon. In reality, the uncertainty comes from disobeying love as too demanding or hard and believing the lie that you are left to yourself.

Absolute love is an eternally passionate commitment to the ultimate benefit of another.

Faith is the characteristic quality of a life that has surrendered to love's purposes for him or her, though unseen and unknown. It includes elements of fear, but it is a certain fear that is convinced that if love is not obeyed it would result in the worst possible existence for him or her.

Primarily the characteristics of faith are humility, belief, trust, acceptance, confidence, gratitude, compassion, freedom, stewardship, servanthood, loyalty, purity, justice, rest, and determination.

End Notes

1. Viscott, David, MD. *Emotional Resilience*. Harmony Books, Crown Publishers, Inc., 1996, page 74.
2. White, Dr. John, *Changing on the Inside*. Ann Arbor, MI, Servant Publications, 1991, page 41.
3. Ibid., pages 58-59.
4. Peck, M. Scott, MD. *The Road Less Traveled and Beyond*. New York, NY, Touchstone Publishing, 1997, page 113-117.
5. DeMarco, Dr. Anthony. *Preemptive Healing*. www.preemptivehealing.com.
6. Ibid.
7. Ibid.
8. Ibid.
9. Goleman, Daniel; Boyazatis, Richard; and McKee, Annie. *Primal Leadership*. Boston, MA, Harvard Business School Press, 2002, page 7.
10. Lewis, C. S. *Mere Christianity*. MacMillan Publishing, New York, N Y, 1943, page 151.
11. Zodhiates, Dr. Spiros. *Complete Word Study Dictionary*. AMG Publishers, Chattanooga, TN, 1994.

of the books agree on this. Yet revelations mysteriously point to a reality of I AM being a community, a unified self in three, an organization (organism) of three coexistent and equal personalities. The mystery begins in the very first words dictated by Moses. Genesis 1:1: "In the beginning, God created the heavens and the earth." The Hebrew word *Elohim* means God, the one God. It is plural in syntax.

Uniquely, Elohim is not dual two but more than two. This is explained by many as a fullness of the one God, yet this still leaves mystery. Even more mystery is added when the Torah relates this: (Genesis 1:26) "Then God said, 'Let us make man in our image, after our likeness.'" Here plural God (plural Elohim), the one God, says, "Let us" (plural) make "in our" (plural) ...

Genesis 1:27: "So God created man in his own image, in the image of God he (singular) created him; male and female he created them." The image of God is here reflected in community, relatedness. Persons are one in kind, essence, and form (man or human) but different in role and function. Likeness that is meant for unity, that is, meant for loving community. Here indeed is a mystery of how being created as community is being created in the likeness of God. Unity of being human does not mean being identical in personality. Likewise God is One, His Oneness does not prohibit a unity of personhood. The persons as one are revealed, yet veiled in mystery.

Peter Toon writes, "The decision by God to create man in his image was an interpersonal decision. Elohim (God in his plurality) ... the decision of the Three. Yet the Three acted as one: 'Elohim created man in his own image; in the image of Elohim he created him' (where the plural noun takes the singular verbs). If God is simply a monad then he cannot be or know personality. To be personal otherness must be present together with oneness; the one must be in relation to others."[6]

"Love is an indefinable term, and its manifestations are both subtle and infinite. But it begins, I believe, with one absolute condition: unlimited liability! As soon as one's liability for another is qualified to any degree, love is diminished by that much,"[7] says Robert Greenleaf.

Personhood is only a reality where there are relations, relatedness and relationships."Wow, what a mystery! The entire Tanakh reveals God in this way, in this construct, often with {(YHWH, Elohim), (I AM, (God Plural) or (the LORD, (God Plural)} followed by a singular verb.

We might ask, "Are there other pointers to this reality?" This conclusion is often a separator for religious people, especially if God and religion are tied to political or cultural fear of separation from culture and family. To be relationally attuned to I AM, though, is the only way to bring cultures together, to unite.

If we want to have relationship with absolute love, we must look beyond cultural, political, and religious boundaries to I AM as revealed to us. Eugene Peterson writes, "The world, in fact, is not as it has been represented to us. Things are not all right as they are, and they are not getting any better. We have been told the lie ever since we can remember: that human beings are basically nice and good ... How we can keep on believing this after so many centuries of evidence to the contrary is difficult to comprehend, but nothing we do or nothing anyone else does to us seems to disenchant us from the spell of the lie."[8]

Petersen writes further, "The lies are impeccably factual. They contain no errors. There are no distortions or falsified data. But they are lies all the same because they claim to tell us who we are and omit everything about our origin in God and our destiny in God. They talk about the world without telling us that God made it."[9]

A world where God is absent is a lie and gives no absolute help to retrieve healthy relationships, to gain community. Likewise, a religion that is tied to political or cultural tradition apart from relationship with I AM is a lie. I am not pointing fingers at anyone; I am talking about all mankind whether Christians, Muslims, or Jews. People from all religious backgrounds (and not merely the religions formerly named) have in the past, and many now, wrapped up their faith in political and cultural fear instead of in the love of I AM.

"If you turn your life over to your own concept of God, how do you know whether that concept is powerful enough? To help me God has to be more than a concept ... No if I am to turn my life over to God, it must be God as he is. Not God as I conceive him, but God as he conceives himself to be. If there is a God then He is a person, not an idea,"[10] writes Dr. John White .

What happened when mankind broke relationship with I AM? We decided we could, apart from relationship with I AM, rightly decide between what was good for us relationally and what was harmful for us relationally. We distort and suppress the truth about ourselves as being unable to be absolutely loving. We have the desire to be loved but not the ability to be absolutely loving.

Absolute love is an eternally passionate commitment to the ultimate benefit of another. This is the love that the organizational personalities of I AM (the three in one) demonstrate to one another. This love overflows from within I AM to all of us, though we all reject this love in many ways. This is the sickness of sin. The ability to fully accept this love was discarded by mankind in the garden. This is the love only an eternal being could grant. This is the relationship lost through the brokenness of community granted by I AM. Love now is temporal and relative, not eternal and absolute. When mankind is separated from I AM, we begin to worship things, created beings, self. Mankind makes idols, and the exchange we have made is from I AM as an overflowing fountain of the glory of loving-kindness, to images of ourselves. We have exchanged abounding, overflowing, steadfast love with idols to our personal, political, and cultural biases.

I AM will not give His glory to another and thereby displace absolute love. "I will by no means clear the guilty" (Exodus 34:7). In that exchange, we idolatrous people do terrible things.

Romans 1:28-32: "And since they did not see fit to acknowledge God, God gave them up to a debased mind to do what ought not to be done. They were filled with all manner of unrighteousness, evil, covetousness, malice. They are full of envy, murder, strife, deceit, maliciousness. They are gossips, slanderers, haters of God, insolent, haughty, boastful, inventors of evil, disobedient to parents, foolish, faithless, heartless, ruthless. Though they know God's decree that those who practice such things deserve to die, they not only do them but give approval to those who practice them." This sounds like the nightly news or, if you like, a television program watched for evening entertainment. This was written two thousand years ago. Would the atheist really ask why an absolutely loving God would decree death and destruction upon evil people? Should we not ask why an absolutely loving God continues to give us the grace of life? This is an absolute blow to the modern cult of intellect, self-esteem, and narcissism, a blow to mankind as the final arbiter of good and evil.

To human beings, I AM says, "You shall not eat of the tree of the knowledge of good and evil." This is I AM's only command, only prescription for life. Someone may ask, "Well, now, in most of the world there is not a lot of idol worship. We don't have people sacrificing their children or virgins to idols like they did in ancient civilizations. We don't have temple prostitutes, men and women, who were enslaved in the service of idol worshippers like they did in the ancient empires. No, today in the modern world we have more sophisticated idolatries; they are still images of self-worship (creature worship).

In the present day, men have found more palatable ways to idolize self. When the philosopher Rene Descartes came to his intellectual end and believed that, through intellectual reasoning there was no absolute reality, his famous dictum of his own absolute reality was uttered: "I think therefore, I am." Man in his own intellectual wisdom cannot come up with a different answer.

In classes on psychology in college and in seminary, the modern idea put forth by the psychologist Abraham Maslow about mankind's hierarchy of needs was put forth. Maslow's hierarchy begins with basic needs of survival (i.e., food and shelter) and crescendos to the top as self-actualization. How novel an idea!

Webster's Dictionary describes self-actualization as "full development of one's abilities." At almost every business seminar and many church seminars, I can remember presenters holding up Maslow's pyramid of man's essential needs as gospel truth about our need, and the proper response to that need, as the rebuilding of self-esteem. The *Baker Encyclopedia of Psychology* describes Maslow's claim in developing the hierarchy, that it "fuses the functional tradition of James and Dewey with the holism of Wertheimer, Goldstein, and Gestalt psychology, as well as the dynamism circumcision nor uncircumcision counts for anything, but only faith working through love." Circumcision is only outward evidence of faith in the Tanakh, but I AM desires love as an outworking of faith.

Faith is the characteristic quality of a life that has surrendered to love's purposes for yourself Though unseen and unknown, it includes elements of fear but it is a certain fear that is convinced that if love is not obeyed it would result in the worst possible existence for you. Primarily the characteristics of faith are humility, belief, trust, acceptance, confidence, gratitude, compassion, freedom, loyalty, justice, servanthood, rest, determination, and purity. I know there is mystery here. Don't let mystery be turned to uncertainty. Faith is steeped in certainty but acknowledges mystery. Absolute love is *the one, the three in one*. They are the one and only absolute to whom all others things are relative. This is mystery, however it is mystery revealed.

End Notes

1. Dossey, Larry, MD. *Healing Words: The Power of Prayer and the Practice of Medicine.* HarperCollins, New York, NY, 1993, pages 179–180.

2. Lewis, C. S. *The Abolition of Man.* MacMillan Publishing Co., Inc., New York, NY, 1947, page 78.

3. Piper, Dr. John. *Desiring God: Confessions of a Christian Hedonist.* Multnomah Publishers, Inc., Sisters, OR, 1986, page 256.

4. Andrews, Edgar. *Who Made God: Searching for a Theory of Everything.* EP Books USA, Carlisle, PA, 2009, page 31.

5. Lewis, C. S. *The Abolition of Man: How Education Develops Man's Sense of Morality.* MacMillan Publishing, New York, NY, 1947, pages 44–45.

6. Toon, Peter. *Our Triune God: A Biblical Portrayal of the Trinity.* A Bridgepoint Book, Victor Books, SP Publications, Inc., Wheaton, IL, 1996 , page 199.

7. Greenleaf, Robert. *Servant Leadership: A Journey into the Nature of Legitimate Power and Greatness.* Paulist Press, San Francisco, CA, 1977, page 38.

8. Peterson, Eugene H. *A Long Obedience in the Same Direction.* Intervarsity Press, Downers Grove, IL, 1980, page 22.

9. Ibid, page 23.

10. White, Dr. John. *Changing on the Inside.* Ann Arbor, MI, Servant Publications, 1991, page 158.

11. Benner, David G. ed. *Baker Encyclopedia of Psychology*. Baker Book House, Grand Rapids, MI, 1985, page 685.

12. Ibid., page 686.

13. Tournier, Dr. Paul. *The Whole Person in a Broken World: A Biblical Remedy for Today's World*. Harper and Row Publishers, New York, Hagerstown, San Francisco and London, 1964, pages 13–15, translation from De'sharmonie de La Vie Moderne, Delachau and Nestle SA, Paris, 1947.

14. Ibid., pages 34–35.

15. Packer, J. I. and Howard, Thomas. *Christianity: The True Humanism*. Word Books, Waco, TX, 1985, pages 31–32.

16. Andrews, Edgar. *Who Made God: Searching for a Theory of Everything*. EP Books USA, Carlisle, PA, 2009, page 141.

17. Piper, Dr. John. *Love Your Enemies: Jesus' Love Command in the Synoptic Gospels and the Early Christian Paraenesis*. Cambridge University Press, paperback edition Baker Book House, Grand Rapids, MI, page 31.

must be compelling. Something must change inside you. The change makes possible the awakening of a compelling sense of its attractiveness. So it is with God. You do not merely decide to love him. Something changes inside you, and as a result he becomes compellingly attractive. His glory—his beauty—compels your admiration and delight. He becomes your supreme treasure. You love him."[3]

Beauty is all around. Aesthetics, beauty, nature, man, creation, the world was made very good. It is marred now, but we can see beauty everywhere. Whether you look to unseen truths, evidenced in cell structure (we humans are made up of over 75 trillion cells), studies in DNA and human genomes (we have about thirty-four thousand genes in our makeup), or study the galaxies and the extent of the universe (over one hundred billion stars in our galaxy and over forty billion known galaxies).

Within our universe and outside there are myriads of awe-inspiring discoveries that have been observed and are being observed. We cannot see them if we are focused on ourselves. The person with a microscope and the person with a telescope both experience awe and unspeakable beauty, intricacy, and aesthetic delights. The person who stands on a high bluff or ten thousand feet above the earth on a mountain and the person who looks upon a newborn baby are often overwhelmed by the sheer and immense majesty of what they look upon. The main common denominator between these things is they make us forget about self. What we experience at such times of awe, wonder, and beauty is not something worked up within us; it is a change that comes over us.

This beauty is what I AM, the three in one, experience at all times and have experienced from eternity. Isaiah 57:15: "For thus says the One who is high and lifted up, who inhabits eternity, whose name is Holy: 'I dwell in the high and holy place, and also with him who is of a contrite and lowly spirit, to revive the spirit of the lowly, and to revive the heart of the contrite.'

Psalm 147:6: "The LORD lifts up the humble; he casts the wicked to the ground."

I AM, the three in one, gives no dwelling thought to distinction of presence, power, place, or perfection of self as the individual persons of the entity that is I AM. The persons are only ever distinct in role or function: sometimes "the word of I AM," sometimes "the messenger of I AM," sometimes "the Spirit of I AM"; or Father, Son, and Holy Spirit; or YHWH Elohim (I AM the three in one). No distinction of presence, power, place or perfection only eternal existence. The individual persons of I AM do not degrade or downgrade themselves; they are simply, only, eternally focused upon one another. The three look fully upon the glory of the others and eternal love overflows outside themselves from the beauty and glory of the others, so that there is no thought of self. This is the essence of humility, healthy God-like humility. 1 Corinthians 13:4–7: "Love is patient and kind; love does not envy or boast; it is not arrogant or rude. It does not insist on its own way; it is not irritable or resentful; it does not rejoice at wrongdoing, but rejoices with the truth. love bears all things, believes all things, hopes all things, endures all things."

This is the image of God, humility displayed in love, that Adam and Eve lost by the rebellion in the garden. Romans 3:23, my own paraphrase: "We all have missed the mark, falling short of displaying the glory of the image of God." We lost the simplicity of this awe-filled beauty, all of us, when we turned away from seeing the love of I AM as the most glorious beauty. The beauty of the image of God is now diminished in us, perverted and marred because we all have taken our eyes off I AM and sought to know what is best on our own. The result is sickness and death. As Dr. Paul Tournier has written, "The reader may object, however, that everybody comes up against difficulties in life- disappointments, remorse, injustice, conflicts—but everybody does not fall ill. The truth is that we all experience functional disturbances in varying degrees of intensity and persistence. If we examine closely the psychological reactions which are interfering with the normality of behavior in a neurotic, we are compelled that they are not of a different kind of our own, but merely more intense: they are still, fear, jealousy, susceptibility, anger, dissimulation, self-pity, sentimentality, erotic desire, and depression. What characterizes the neurotic is the fact that the very intensity of his reactions sets up a vicious circle from which he is unable to escape on his own."[4]

Psychology may be somewhat helpful to restore function to being less interruptive, but the answers of theories of psychology must still be presented as practice, as medicine, and all sciences must be considered as practice and theory, not absolute reality. In *Modern Psychotherapies* the authors note, "A recent work indentified 260 distinct schools of psychotherapy."[5]

Maslow's hierarchy of needs must be turned on its head. I am amazed at how many people who have nothing in this world are happy with family, friends, and God. They find the beauty of relational love. I am equally taken back by how many learned, wealthy, *self-sufficient* people are discontent, unhappy, and self-absorbed.

The thrill of viewing the wonders of God's nature as awesome and beautiful, full of wonder, whether viewing though microscope, telescope, or standing on the crest of a hill is lost on material junk. In viewing to see the various and resplendent pointers to the creator, I AM, we begin to open up our sense and develop a sense of awe in God. Finally allowing that beauty to be contemplated in the revelations of I AM in the life of Yeshua, Isa, Jesus of Nazareth culminates in worship-doxology.

The habit, the folly, the missing of the mark is hard to break away from. We are captivated by our choice to turn to ourselves. We are trapped by turning to worshiping the creation rather that the creator. Scientists rely on their intellectual prowess and devise ways to raise their standing in the scientific community. Religious followers set up outward idols and meaningless religious activity in order to build standing among other religious followers. In the midst of this is the stench of death. How will we be freed from the curse of establishing our own knowledge of good and evil? Romans 6:23, my own paraphrase: "How you get rewarded by missing the mark is death (the ever more difficult task of establishing glory for yourself), however God's free gift (fellowship with I AM), is perpetual abundant living which is found in Christ Jesus the I AM." Amazingly, wonderfully beautiful, this perpetual abundant happens to us by looking at, learning of, following after I AM—Yeshua, Isa, Jesus.

Paul Tournier says, "What remains of genuineness to our life is what comes from God and not from ourselves, from His grace and not from our own merits. This may be the appropriate but humiliating return to oneself to which He leads us by psychoanalysis. God has dealings with us: He speaks to us: He acts within us and lays hold of us. When this is experienced we know there is genuineness, the sole genuine content, which alone is of vale and is sufficient for us, and that we can now abandon all those values by which we thought to gain merit before Him."[6]

Tournier later says, "Anyone who claims to love without limit does not know what love is; for one who knows it truly admits that he is incapable of it. But this, behavior of patients shows the vital need we all have of finding something absolute upon which we can count absolutely, something unfailing which gives the lie to all the relativities life teaches us through many sufferings, wherein every trust has its limits, every hope its disappointments, every friendship its eclipse. The absolute is God; and what our patients are looking for when they put us to the test ... is at least some reflection of God, of a love which goes beyond mere convention; and it is roof that they all seek God, even without knowing it."[7]

The beginning of returning to love, of learning from and looking to I AM, is humility. Humility, of course—it is said that as soon as you believe you have achieved it you have lost it. This is a misunderstanding of humility, the humility that I AM displays. Humility in I AM, the three in one, is the overflow of love between the persons who look upon one another and are not focused on themselves. This humility allows them to give and receive from each other. The Father gives and receives from the Son. The Son gives and receives from the Father. Both the Father and Son give and receive from the Spirit. Giving and receiving, looking only at the other and not self, overflows through love, in creation, and also to sustaining the creation. This is the special love of I AM displayed by mercy.

I AM says (Matthew 11:28) "Come to me, all who labor and are heavy laden, and I will give you rest." James 4:1-10 "What causes quarrels and what causes fights among you? Is it not this, that your passions are at war within you? You desire and do not have, so you murder. You covet however, they express the continually renewed, because continually necessary, attempt to negate that misconception of ourselves and of our relation to God which nature, even while we pray, is always recommending to us. No sooner do we believe that God loves us than there is an impulse to believe that He does so, not because He is love, but because we are intrinsically lovable. The Pagans obeyed this impulse unabashed; a good man was 'dear to the gods' because he was good. We, being better taught, resort to subterfuge. Far be it from us to think that we have virtues for which God could love us. But then, how magnificently we have repented! As Bunyan says, describing his first illusory conversion, 'I thought there was no man in England that pleased God better than I.' Beaten out of this, we next offer our own humility to God's admiration. Surely He'll like that? Or if not that, our clear-sighted and humble recognition that we still lack humility. Thus, depth beneath depth and subtlety within subtlety, there remains some lingering idea of our own, our very own, attractiveness. It is easy to acknowledge, but almost impossible to realize for long, that we are mirrors whose brightness, if we are bright, is wholly derived from the sun that shines upon us. Surely we must have a little—however little— native luminosity? Surely we can't be quite creatures.

"For this tangled absurdity of a Need. Even a Need-love, which never fully acknowledges its own neediness, Grace substitutes a full, childlike and delighted acceptance of our Need, a joy in total dependence. We become 'jolly beggars.' The good man is sorry for the sins which have increased his Need. He is not entirely sorry for the fresh Need they have produced. And he is not sorry at all for the innocent Need that is inherent in his creaturely condition. For all the time this illusion to which nature clings as her last treasure, this pretence that we have anything of our own or could for one hour retain by our own strength any goodness that God may pour into us, has kept us from being happy. We have been like bathers who want to keep their feet-or one foot-or one toe-on the bottom, when to lose that foothold would be to surrender themselves to a glorious tumble in the surf. The consequences of parting with our last claim to intrinsic freedom, power, or worth, are real freedom, power and worth, really ours just because God gives them and because we know them to be (in another sense) not 'ours' ...

'But God also transforms our Need-love for one another, and it requires equal transformation. In reality we all need at times, some of us at most times, that Charity from others which, being Love Himself in them, loves the unlovable. But this, though a sort of love we need, is not the sort we want. We want to be loved for our cleverness, beauty, generosity, fairness, usefulness. The first hint that anyone is offering us the highest love of all is a terrible shock. This is so well recognized that spiteful people will pretend to be loving us with Charity precisely because they know that it will wound us. To say to one who expects a renewal of Affection, Friendship, or Eros, 'I forgive you as a Christian' is merely a way of continuing the quarrel. Those who say it are of course lying. But the thing would not be falsely said in order to wound unless, if it were true, it would be wounding.

"How difficult it is to receive, and to go on receiving from others a love that does not depend on our own attraction can be seen from an extreme case. Suppose yourself a man struck down shortly after marriage by an incurable disease which may not kill you for years; useless, impotent, hideous disgusting; dependent on your wife's earnings; impoverishing where you hoped to enrich; impaired even in intellect and shaken by gusts of uncontrollable temper, full of unavoidable demands. And suppose your wife's care and pity to be inexhaustible. The man who can take this sweetly, who can receive all and give nothing without resentment, who can abstain even from those tiresome self-depreciations which are really a demand for petting and reassurance, is doing something which Need-love in its merely natural condition could not attain ... But what the extreme example illustrates is universal. We are all receiving Charity. There is something in each of us that cannot be naturally loved. It is no one's fault if they do not so love it. Only the lovable can be naturally loved. You might as well ask people to like the taste of rotten bread or the sound of a mechanical drill. We can be forgiven, and pitied, and loved in spite of it, with Charity; no other way. All who have good parents, wives, husbands, or children, may be sure that at times-and perhaps at all times in respect of some one particular trait or habit- they are receiving Charity, are loved not because they are lovable but because Love Himself is in those who love them."[9]

Humility is the beginning of faith that love works in us as we look outside ourselves to I AM. Humility involves being able to give to others but also to receive from others as we keep our eyes fixed on I AM and thereby become more like Him in love. The key element of humility is mercifulness. Isa Al-Masih, Yeshua born of the lineage of David, Jesus of Nazareth, said in Matthew 5:3, "Blessed are the poor in spirit, for theirs is the kingdom of heaven."

Aniy (humble, poor, afflicted, weak, lowly) Exodus 22:25, Leviticus 19:10, 23:22, Deuteronomy 15:11, 24:12, 24:14, 24:15, 2 Samuel 22:28, Job 24:9, 24:14, 29:12, 34:28, 36:6, 36:15, Psalm 9:12, 9:18, 10:2, 10:9, 10:12, **10:17**, 12:5, 14:6, 18:27, 22:24, 25:16, 34:2, 34:6, 35:10, 37:14, 40:17, 68:10, 69:29, 69:32, 70:5, 72:2, 72:4, 72:12, 74:19, 74:21, 82:3, 86:1, 88:15, 102:1, 109:16, 109:22, 140:12, Proverbs 3:34, 14:2, 15:15, 16:19, 22:22, 30:14, 31:9, 31:20, Ecclesiastes 6:8, Isaiah 3:14, 3:15, 10:2, 10:30, 14:32, 26:6, 32:7, 41:17, 49:13, 51:21, 54:11, 58:7, 66:2, Jeremiah 22:16, Ezekiel 16:49, 18:12, 18:17, 22:29, Amos 8:4, Habakkuk 3:14, Zephaniah 3:12, Zechariah 7:10, 9:9, 11:7, 11:11 **Anav** (humble, meek, needy, poor) **Numbers 12:3**, Job 24:4, Psalm 9:18, 22:26, **25:9, 37:11**, 76:9, 147:6, 149:4, Proverbs 14:21, Isaiah 11:4, 29:19, 32:7, 61:1, Amos 2:7, 8:4, Zephaniah 2:3 **Anavah** (humility) Psalm 18:35, Proverbs 15:33, 18:12, 22:4, Zephaniah 2:3, **Anah** (bowed down, afflicted, humble) Genesis 15:13, 16:6, 16:9, 31:50, 34:2, Exodus 1:11, 1:12, 10:3, 22:22, 22:23, 32:18, Leviticus 16:29, 16:31, 23:27, 23:29, 23:32, Numbers 24:24, 29:7, 30:13, **Deuteronomy 8:2, 8:3, 8:16**, 21:14, 22:24, 22:29, 26:6, Judges 16:5, 16:6, 16:19, 19:24, 20:5, 2 Samuel 7:10, 13:12, 13:14, 13:22, 13:32, 22:36, 1 Kings 2:26, 8:35, 11:39, 2 Kings 17:20, 2 Chronicles 6:26, Ezra 8:21, Job 30:11, 37:23, Psalm 35:13, 55:19, 88:7, 89:22, 90:15, 94:5, 102:23, 105:18, 107:17, 116:10, **119:67, 119:71, 119:75, 119:107**, 132:1, Ecclesiastes 1:13, 3:10, Isaiah 27:2, 31:4, 53:4, 53:7, **58:3, 58:5, 58:10**, 60:14, 64:12, Lamentations 3:33, 5:11, Ezekiel 22:10, 22:11, **Daniel 10:12**, Nahum 1:12, Zephaniah 3:19, Zechariah 10:2.

Tapeinos (humble, low, undistinguished, pliant, bow down, modest) **Matthew 11:29**, Luke 1:52, Romans 12:16, 2 Corinthians 7:6, 10:1, James 1:9, 4:6, 1 Peter 5:5 **Tapeinophrosune** Acts 20:19, ph 4:2, **Phil 2:3**, Colossians 2:18, 2:23, 3:12, 1 Peter 5:5, **Tapeinoo** Matthew 18:4, 23:12, Luke 3:5, 14:11, 18:14, 2 Corinthians 11:7, 12:21, **Phil 2:7, 2:8**, 4:12, **James 4:10, 1 Peter 5:6 Tapeinosis** Luke 1:48, Acts 8:33, Phil 3:21, James 1:10.

End Notes

1. Morris, Leon. *Testaments of Love: A Study of love in the Bible.* Wm. B. Eerdmans Publishing Co., Grand Rapids, MI, 1981, page 25.
2. Benner, David G. ed. *Baker Encyclopedia of Psychology.* Baker Book House, Grand Rapids, MI, 1985, page 685.
3. Piper, Dr. John. *Think: The Life of the Mind and the Love of God.* Desiring God Foundation, Crossway Publishers, Wheaton, IL, 2010, pages 86, 87.
4. Tournier, Dr. Paul. *The Healing of Persons.* Harper and Row Publishers, New York, NY, 1965, page 46.
5. Jones, Stanton L.; and Butman, Richard E. *Modern Psychotherapies.* Intervarsity Press, Downers Grove, IL, 1991, page 11.
6. Tournier, Dr. Paul. *Guilt and Grace: A Psychological Study.* Harper and Row Publishers, New York, Evanston and London, 1969, page 131, English translation by Arthur W. Hethcote, asst. by J. J. Henry and P. J. Allcock, originally published Switzerland, 1958, Delachaux and Nestle.
7. Ibid., page 193.
8. McBrien, Richard P. *Catholicism.* Christianity Today, www.ctlibrary.com, January 8, 1996.
9. Lewis, C. S. *The Four Loves: In the Inspirational Writings of C. S. Lewis.* Inspirational Press, New York, NY, 1960, by Helen Joy Lewis, pages 283-284.

CHAPTER SIX

Belief and Trust

When mankind denies there is a God, or replaces I AM, the three in one, with a created or imagined substitute, truth is suppressed psychologically and emotions are repressed. The outcome of suppressing the truth is living a lie, being ashamed, and hiding from truth. Genesis 3:7-10: "Then the eyes of both were opened, and they knew that they were naked. And they sewed fig leaves together and made themselves loincloths. And they heard the sound of the LORD God walking in the garden in the cool of the day, and the man and his wife hid themselves from the presence of the LORD God among the trees of the garden. But the LORD God called to the man and said to him, 'Where are you?' And he said, 'I heard the sound of you in the garden, and I was afraid, because I was naked, and I hid myself.'

David Wells writes, "It is no coincidence, then that this generation knows a lot about failed relationships and has experienced the moral ambiguity that modern culture inflicts upon those who feast at its table. For this generation, in particular, codependency groups and twelve step programs have offered the way out. They provide relationships, a community, and people who will listen- and a safe environment ...

"In these groups it is assumed, and often explicitly stated, that our innate drives tend not toward destruction, but toward growth, health and happiness; and that society is burdensome and oppressive to the self ... The inevitable outcome of treating the self as the locus of meaning and of all moral values, however, is that both meaning and values become relative to each self. If self-consciousness is private, unique and individualized, then moral values, if they arise in the self, are as private and individualized as the self in which they reside. A sense of responsibility toward anyone outside the self dies, as does integrity- that moral quality which secures continuity between what is said or done in one moment and what is said or done in the future."[1]

The outcome of repressed emotions is an inner upheaval that rebels against us physically and emotionally in pain and in a darkened, deadened, perverted mind or process of thought. Instead of lifting up our worth as created in the image of I AM, we relate worth to subjective thought and perceived beneficial activity. Paradoxically, lifting up self invites us to devalue other people and more often than not devalue ourselves. Looking away from ourselves, outward to love I AM and love others, forgetting self. Mark 12:29-31: "Jesus answered, 'The most important is, 'Hear, O Israel: The Lord our God, the Lord is one. And you shall love the Lord your God with all your heart and with all your soul and with all your mind and with all your strength.' The second is this: 'You shall love your neighbor as yourself.' There is no other commandment greater than these.'"

The setting up of our own idea of health and happiness has been the greatest failure to achieve what we seek as mankind. Richard Keyes says, "Idolatry may not involve explicit denials of God's existence or character. It may well come in the form of over attachment to something that is, in itself, perfectly good. The crucial warning is this: As soon as our loyalty to anything else leads us to disobey God, we are in danger of making it an idol.

"As we will see, an idol need not be a full-sized replacement for God, for nothing can be. An Idol is something or someone we become increasingly attached to until it comes between us and God, making God remote and His commandments irrelevant or unrealistically prohibitive. In this society, our idols tend to be in clusters. They are inflationary, have short shelf lives, change, adapt, and multiply quickly as if by mitosis, or cell division. An idol can be a physical object, a property, a person, an activity, a role, an institution, a hope, an image, a pleasure, a hero—anything that can substitute for God ...

"To summarize, idols will inevitably involve self-centeredness, self-inflation and self deception. Idolatry begins with counterfeiting of God, because only with a counterfeit God can people remain the center of their lives and loyalties, autonomous architects of their futures ... But a counterfeit is a lie, not the real thing. It must present itself through self-deception, often with images suggesting that the idol will fulfill promises for the good life."[2]

In our pursuit of happiness, we look outside of ourselves in humility. Humility is the first step on the way to love. We as creatures look to I AM as our creator to find fulfillment the kind of joy and happiness that doesn't come from anything outside of Him. Likewise, I AM looks only within Himself to find, happiness, love, fulfillment.

John Piper writes, "How we view God will determine our idea of how we can please God. And how a person decides to try to please God is the most fateful decision a person can ever make. What if you discovered (like the Pharisees did), that you had devoted your whole life to trying to please God, but all the while you had been doing things that in God's sight were abominations (Luke 16:14-15)? Someone may say, 'I don't think that's possible; God wouldn't reject a person who has been trying to please him.' But do you see what the questioner has done? He has based his conviction about what would please God on His idea of what God is like. That is precisely why we must begin with the character of God. That is why we begin with the pleasures of God in Himself ...

"God has no deficiencies that I might be required to supply. He is complete in himself. He is overflowing with happiness in the fellowship of the Trinity. The upshot of this is that God is a mountain spring, not a watering trough. A mountain spring is self-replenishing. It constantly overflows and supplies others. But a watering trough needs to be filled with a pump or bucket brigade. So if you want to glorify the worth of the watering rough you work hard to keep it full and useful. But if you want to glorify the worth of the spring you do it by getting down on your hands and knees and drinking to your heart's satisfaction, until you have the refreshment and strength to go back down in the valley and tell the people what you've found. You do not glorify a mountain spring by dutifully hauling water up the path from the river below and dumping it in the spring. What we have seen is God is like a mountain spring, not a watering trough. And since God is the way God is, we are not surprised to learn from Scripture- and our faith is strengthened to hold fast—that the way to please God is to come to him to get and not to give, to drink and not to water. He is most glorified in us when we are most satisfied in him.

"My hope as a desperate sinner, who lives in a Death Valley desert of unrighteousness, hangs on this biblical truth that Gods the kind of God who will be pleased with the one thing I have to offer- my thirst. That is why the sovereign freedom and self-sufficiency of God are so precious to me: they arc the foundation of my hope that God is delighted not by the resourcefulness of bucket brigades, but by the bending down of broken sinner to drink at the fountain of grace ...

"In other words, this unspeakable good news for helpless sinners- that God delights not when we offer him our strength but when we wait for his- this good news that I need to hear so badly again and again, is based firmly on a vision of God as sovereign, self-sufficient and free. If we do not have this foundational vision of God in place when we ask how we can please him, it is almost certain that our efforts to please him will become subtle means of self-exaltation, and end in the oppressive bondage of legalistic strivings."[3]

Jonathan Edwards, in an unpublished essay on the Trinity, lays out for us a clear picture of how the one God, I AM, is perfectly content in the belief and trust of Himself.

> And this I suppose to be that blessed Trinity that we read of in the Holy Scriptures. The Father is the Deity subsisting in the prime, un-originated and most absolute manner, or the Deity in its direct existence. The Son is the Deity generated by God's understanding, or having

an idea of Himself and subsisting in that idea. The Holy Ghost is the Deity subsisting in act, or the Divine essence flowing out and breathed forth in God's Infinite love to and delight in Himself. And I believe the whole Divine essence does truly and distinctly subsist both in the Divine idea and Divine love, and that each of them are properly distinct Persons ...

Hereby we see how the Father is the fountain of the Godhead, and why when He is spoken of in Scripture He is so often, without any addition or distinction, called God, which has led some to think that He only was truly and properly God. Hereby we may see why in the economy of the Persons of the Trinity the Father should sustain the dignity of the Deity, that the Father should have it as His office to uphold and maintain the rights of the Godhead and should be God not only by essence, but as it were, by His economical office. Hereby is illustrated the doctrine of the Holy Ghost. Proceeding [from] both the Father and the Son. Hereby we see how that it is possible for the Son to be begotten by the Father and the Holy Ghost to proceed from the Father and Son, and yet that all the Persons should be Co-eternal. Hereby we may more clearly understand the equality of the Persons among themselves, and that they are every way equal in the society or family of the three.

They are equal in honor: besides the honor which is common to them all, viz., that they are all God, each has His peculiar honor in the society or family. They are equal not only in essence, but the Father's honor is that He is, as it were, the Author of perfect and Infinite wisdom. The Son's honor is that He is that perfect and Divine wisdom itself the excellency of which is that from whence arises the honor of being the author or Generator of it. The honor of the Father and the Son is that they are infinitely excellent, or that from them infinite excellency proceeds; but the honor of the Holy Ghost is equal for He is that Divine excellency and beauty itself. 'Tis the honor of the Father and the Son that they are infinitely holy and are the fountain of holiness, but the honor of the Holy Ghost is that holiness itself. The honor of the Father and the Son is [that] they are infinitely happy and are the original and fountain of happiness and the honor of the Holy Ghost is equal for He is infinite happiness and joy itself.

The honor of the Father is that He is the fountain of the Deity as He from Whom proceed both the Divine wisdom and also excellency and happiness. The honor of the Son is equal for He is Himself the Divine wisdom and is He from Whom proceeds the Divine excellency and happiness, and the honor of the Holy Ghost is equal for He is the beauty and happiness of both the other Persons.

By this also we may fully understand the equality of each Person's concern in the work of redemption, and the equality of the Redeemed's concern with them and dependence upon them, and the equality and honor and praise due to each of them. Glory belongs to the Father and the Son that they so greatly loved the world: to the Father that He so loved that He gave His Only Begotten Son: to the Son that He so loved the world as to give up Himself.

But there is equal glory due to the Holy Ghost for He is that love of the Father and the Son to the world. Just so much as the two first Persons glorify themselves by showing the astonishing greatness of their love and grace, just so much is that wonderful love and grace glorified Who is the Holy Ghost. It shows the Infinite dignity and excellency of the Father that the Son so delighted and prized His honor and glory that He stooped infinitely low rather than [that] men's salvation should be to the injury of that honor and glory.

It showed the infinite excellency and worth of the Son that the Father so delighted in Him that for His sake He was ready to quit His anger and receive into favor those that had [deserved?] infinitely ill at His Hands, and what was done shows how great the excellency and worth of the Holy Ghost

Who is that delight which the Father and the Son have in each other: it shows it to be Infinite. So great as the worth of a thing delighted in is to any one, so great is the worth of that delight and joy itself which he has in it.

Our dependence is equally upon each in this office. The Father appoints and provides the Redeemer, and Himself accepts the price and grants the thing purchased; the Son is the Redeemer by offering Himself and is the price; and the Holy Ghost immediately communicates to us the thing purchased by communicating Himself, and He is the thing purchased. The sum of all that Christ purchased for men was the Holy Ghost. Galatians. 3:13, 14: "He was made a curse for us ... that we might receive the promise of the Spirit through faith."

What Christ purchased for us was that we have communion with God [which] is His good, which consists in partaking of the Holy Ghost: as we have shown, all the blessedness of the Redeemed consists in their partaking of Christ's fullness, which consists in partaking of that Spirit which is given not by measure unto him: the oil that is poured on the head of the Church runs down to the members of His body and to the skirts of His garment (Psalm 133:2). Christ purchased for us that we should have the favor of God and might enjoy His love, but this love is the Holy Ghost.

Christ purchased for us true spiritual excellency, grace and holiness, the sum of which is love to God, which is [nothing] but the indwelling of the Holy Ghost in the heart. Christ purchased for us spiritual joy and comfort, which is in a participation of God's joy and happiness, which joy and happiness is the Holy Ghost as we have shown. The Holy Ghost is the sum of all good things. Good things and the Holy Spirit are synonymous expressions in Scripture: (Matthew 7:11) "How much more shall your Heavenly Father give the Holy Spirit to them that ask Him." The sum of all spiritual good which the finite have in this world is that spring of living water within them which we read of (John 4:10), and those rivers of living water flowing out of them which we read of (John 7:38, 39), which we are there told means the Holy Ghost; and the sum of all happiness in the other world is that river of water of life which proceeds out of the throne of God and the Lamb, which we read of (Revelation 22:1), which is the River of God's pleasures and is the Holy Ghost and therefore the sum of the Gospel invitation to come and take the water of life (verse 17).

The Holy Ghost is the purchased possession and inheritance of the saints, as appears because that little of it which the saints have in this world is said to be the earnest of that purchased inheritance.

(Ephesians. 1:14) Tis an earnest of that which we are to have a fullness of hereafter. (2 Corinthians 1:22; 5:5) The Holy Ghost is the great subject of all Gospel promises and therefore is called the Spirit of promise.

(Ephesians. 1:13) This is called the promise of the Father (Luke 24:49), and the like in other places. (If the Holy Ghost be a comprehension of all good things promised in the Gospel, we may easily see the force of the Apostle's arguing (Galatians. 3:2), "This only would I know, Received ye the Spirit by the works of the law or by the hearing of faith?") So that it is God of Whom our good is purchased and it is God that purchases it and it is God also that is the thing purchased.

Thus all our good things are of God and through God and in God, as we read in Romans 11:36: "For of Him and through Him and to Him (or in Him as *eis* is rendered, I Corinthians. 8:6) are all things." "To Whom be glory forever." All our good is of God the Father, it is all through God the Son, and all is in the Holy Ghost as He is Himself all our good. God is Himself the portion and purchased inheritance of His people. Thus God is the Alpha and the Omega in this affair of redemption.

If we suppose no more than used to be supposed about the Holy Ghost, the concern of the Holy Ghost in the work of redemption is not equal with the Father's and the Son's, nor is there an equal part of the glory of this work belonging to Him: merely to apply to us or immediately to give or hand to us the blessing purchased, after it was purchased, as subservient to the other two Persons, is but a little thing [compared] to the purchasing of it by the paying an Infinite price, by Christ offering up Himself in sacrifice to procure it, and it is but a little thing to God the Father's giving His infinitely dear Son to be a sacrifice for us and upon His purchase to afford to us all the blessings of His purchased.

But according to this there is an equality. To be the love of God to the world is as much as for the Father and the Son to do so much from love to the world, and to be the thing purchased was as much as to be the price. The price and the thing bought with that price are equal. And it is as much as to afford the thing purchased, for the glory that belongs to Him that affords the thing purchased arises from the worth of that thing that He affords and therefore it is the same glory and an equal glory; the glory of the thing itself is its worth and that is also the glory of him that affords it.

There are two more eminent and remarkable images of the Trinity among the creatures. The one is in the spiritual creation, the soul of man. There is the mind, and the understanding or idea, and the spirit of the mind as it is called in Scripture, i.e., the disposition, the will or affection. The other is in the visible creation, viz., the Sun. The father is as the substance of the Sun. (By substance I don't mean in a philosophical sense, but the Sun as to its internal constitution.) The Son is as the brightness and glory of the disk of the Sun or that bright and glorious form under which it appears to our eyes. The Holy Ghost is the action of the Sun which is within the Sun in its intestine heat, and, being diffusive, enlightens, warms, enlivens and comforts the world. The

have been involved in enabling, scapegoating, stereotyping, and other sinful behaviors that inhibit and destroy our relationship with I AM and with those around us. The mercy, loving kindness and forgiveness of I AM can release us from those so that we can believe in ourselves and others.

It is then necessary to see that belief and trust mainly flow through looking to and passionately abiding in I AM. This is where we fail to love God and love others as ourselves, as Adam and Eve failed. We can only believe and trust in ourselves to the extent that we keep focus on I AM. One of the greatest truths the best psychiatrists and psychologists know is that we have an unceasing ability to deceive ourselves, to hide and distort truth. Psychology did not first discover this fact, though it is revealed through the study of the nature of man—I AM revealed this. Of Jesus of Nazareth, I AM incarnate, it is revealed in John 2:23-25, "Now when he was in Jerusalem at the Passover Feast, many believed in his name when they saw the signs that he was doing. But Jesus on his part did not entrust himself to them, because he knew all people and needed no one to bear witness about man, for he himself knew what was in man."

Yeshua, Jesus, Isa is the Word (I AM, the three in one). Yet He lived as a Jewish man (the Messiah or anointed one) who affirmed celebrating Passover (indeed it was a celebration of Himself and His coming substitutionary sacrifice), yet love for others flowed from belief and trust in the Father (I AM, the three in one) and The Holy Spirit (I AM, the three in one). He was not entrusting himself to man. He knew what was in mankind: deception and hiding. He was believing and trusting in the Father and the Holy Spirit.

Other encounters in the life of Jesus record how even enemies of I AM can desire the blessings and benefits of I AM without wanting to live in intimate relationship with Him. We often want to reduce faith and love to temporal satisfaction without seeing the benefit of turning away from everything else to only looking to I AM.

A young man of the ruling class in Palestine once came to Jesus looking to hold on to everything else and still have the benefit and blessing of I AM. Luke 18:18-27: "And a ruler asked him, 'Good Teacher, what must I do to inherit eternal life?' And Jesus said to him, 'Why do you call me good? No one is good except God alone. You know the commandments: 'Do not commit adultery, Do not murder, Do not steal, Do not bear false witness, Honor your father and mother.' And he said, 'All these I have kept from my youth.' When Jesus heard this, he said to him, 'One thing you still lack. Sell all that you have and distribute to the poor, and you will have treasure in heaven; and come, follow me.' But when he heard these things, he became very sad, for he was extremely rich. Jesus, seeing that he had become sad, said, 'How difficult it is for those who have wealth to enter the kingdom of God! For it is easier for a camel to go through the eye of a needle than for a rich person to enter the kingdom of God.' Those who heard it said, 'Then who can be saved?' But he said, 'What is impossible with men is possible with God.'"

It is totally turning away from self to I AM that allows us to really live, to have abundant, eternal life. This kind of life is only from I AM not from ourselves. "The deepest healing occurs not in the mind, but in the soul. And if the heart is 'hardened,' no words can penetrate it,"[4] writes M. Scott Peck, MD.

In another place, it is revealed Jesus was with those who had given up everything to follow after Him. Matthew 14:22: "Immediately he made the disciples get into the boat and go before him to the other side, while he dismissed the crowds.

> Matthew 14:23-33: And after he had dismissed the crowds, he went up on the mountain by himself to pray. When evening came, he was there alone, but the boat by this time was a long way from the land, beaten by the waves, for the wind was against them. And in the fourth watch of the night he came to them, walking on the sea. But when the disciples saw him walking on the sea, they were terrified, and said, "It is a ghost!" and they cried out in fear. But immediately Jesus spoke to them, saying, "Take heart; it is I. Do not be afraid." And Peter answered him, "Lord, if it is you, command me to come to you on

the water." He said, "Come." So Peter got out of the boat and walked on the water and came to Jesus. But when he saw the wind, he was afraid, and beginning to sink he cried out, "Lord, save me." Jesus immediately reached out his hand and took hold of him, saying to him, "O you of little faith, why did you doubt?" And when they got into the boat, the wind ceased. And those in the boat worshiped him, saying, "Truly you are the Son of God."

Even those who are seen as most in touch with and focused on God can fail when they take their eyes off I AM. This should be a strong warning to us not to be thrown off by failures of others and then to let those failures of man to cause us to lose belief and trust in God.

Yet again another encounter with Jesus should help us to see that our perception should not be the basis of belief and trust. Jesus had been teaching across the land and healing many people from Israel. Then he was approached by a Roman soldier, a centurion. Matthew 8:5-13:

When he entered Capernaum, a centurion came forward to him, appealing to him, "Lord, my servant is lying paralyzed at home, suffering terribly." And he said to him, "I will come and heal him." But the centurion replied, "Lord, I am not worthy to have you come under my roof, but only say the word, and my servant will be healed. For I too am a man under authority, with soldiers under me. And I say to one, 'Go,' and he goes, and to another, 'Come,' and he comes, and to my servant, 'Do this,' and he does it." When Jesus heard this, he marveled and said to those who followed him, "Truly, I tell you, with no one in Israel have I found such faith. I tell you, many will come from east and west and recline at table with Abraham, Isaac, and Jacob in the kingdom of heaven, while the sons of the kingdom will be thrown into the outer darkness. In that place there will be weeping and gnashing of teeth." And to the centurion Jesus said, "Go; let it be done for you as you have believed." And the servant was healed at that very moment.

Often those who we believe to be enemies or those who we think are outside of the focus of I AM are exactly the opposite: they are more clearly focused on I AM or at least have the potential to be focused on I AM. As we have already seen with man, this is impossible, but with God all things are possible. This is the dilemma of trying to go it without God—it brings impossibility, it brings death. Hence as I AM teaches, we should love our enemies. Matthew 5:38–48: "You have heard that it was said, 'An eye for an eye and a tooth for a tooth.' But I say to you, Do not resist the one who is evil. But if anyone slaps you on the right cheek, turn to him the other also. And if anyone would sue you and take your tunic, let him have your cloak as well. And if anyone forces you to go one mile, go with him two miles. Give to the one who begs from you, and do not refuse the one who would borrow from you. "You have heard that it was said, 'You shall love your neighbor and hate your enemy.' But I say to you, love your enemies and pray for those who persecute you, so that you may be sons of your Father who is in heaven. For he makes his sun rise on the evil and on the good, and sends rain on the just and on the unjust. For if you love those who love you, what reward do you have? Do not even the tax collectors do the same?" And if you greet only your brothers, what more are you doing than others? Do not even the Gentiles do the same? You therefore must be perfect, as your heavenly Father is perfect."

To be focused on I AM is to follow Him and mirror His character. This is the essence of absolute love. It is love that flows from within the one who loves, not love, that is generated from the loveliness of the object to which love overflows toward. This is the way the absolute love within I AM has been poured out to us. Romans 5:6–11: "For while we were still weak, at the right time Christ died for the ungodly. For one will scarcely die for a righteous person—though perhaps for a good person one would dare even to die— but God shows his love for us in that while we were still sinners, Christ died for us. Since, therefore, we have now

2 Samuel 4:4, 7:16, 20:19, 1 Kings 8:26, 10:7, 11:38, 2 Kings 10:1, 10:5, 17:14, 1 Chronicles 17:23, 17:24, 2 Chronicles 1:9, 6:17, 9:6, 20:20, 32:15, Nehemiah 9:8, 13:13, Esther 2:7, 2:20, Job 4:18, 9:16, 12:20, 15:15, 15:22, 15:31, 24:22, 29:24, 39:12, 39:24, Psalm 12:1, 19:7, 27:13, 31:23, 78:22, 78:32, 89:28, 89:37, 93:5, 101:6, 106:12, 106:24, 111:7, 116:10, 119:66, Proverbs 8:30, 11:13, 14:15, 25:13, 26:25, 27:6, Isaiah 1:21, 1:26, 7:9, 8:2, 22:23, 22:25, 28:16, 33:16, 43:10, 49:7, 49:23, 53:1, 55:3, 60:4, Jeremiah 12:6, 15:18, 40:14, 42:5, Lamentations 4:5, 4:12, Hosea 5:9, 11:12, Jonah 3:5, Micah 7:5, Habakkuk 1:5.

Batach (trust, extend, lie face down, lie down extended, secure, rely upon, and be confident.)

Deuteronomy 28:52, Judges 9:26, 18:7, 18:10, 18:27, 20:36, 2 Kings 18:5, 18:19, 18:20, 18:21, 18:22, 18:24, 18:30, 19:10, 1 Chronicles 5:20, 2 Chronicles 32:10, Job 6:20, 11:18, 39:11, 40:23, Psalm 4:5, 9:10, **13:5, 21:7,** 22:4, 22:5, 22:9, 25:2, 26:1, 27:3, 28:7, 31:6, 31:14, **32:10,** 33:21, 37:3, 37:5, 40:3, 41:9, 44:6, 49:6, **52:7, 52:8,** 55:23, 56:3, 56:4, 56:11, 62:8, 62:10, 78:22, 84:12, 86:2, 91:2, 112:7, 115:8, 115:9, 115:10, 115:11, 118:8, 118:9, 119:42, 125:1, 135:18, **143:8,** 146:3, Proverbs 3:5, 11:15, 11:28, 14:16, 16:20, 28:1, 28:25, 28:26, 29:25, 31:11, Isaiah 12:2, **26:3,** 26:4, 30:12, 31:1, 32:9, 32:10, 32:11, 36:4, 36:5, 36:6, 36:7, 36:9, 36:15, 37:10, 42:17, 47:10, 50:10, 59:4, Jeremiah 5:17, 7:4, 7:8, 7:14, 9:4, 12:5, 13:25, 17:5, 17:7, 28:15, 29:31, 39:18, 46:25, 48:7, 49:4, 49:11, Ezekiel 16:15, 33:13, Hosea 10:13, Amos 6:1, Micah 7:5, Habakkuk 2:18, Zephaniah 3:2.

Pistueo (believe, be convinced of, give credence to, be influenced by.)

Matthew 8:13, 9:28, 18:6, 21:22, 21:25, 21:32, 24:23, 24:26, 27:42, Mark 1:15, 5:36, 9:23, 9:24, 9:42, 11:23, 11:24, 11:31, 13:21, 15:32, 16:13, 16:14, 16:16, 16:17, Luke 1:20, 1:45, 8:12, 8:13, 8:50, 16:11, 20:5, 22:67, 24:25, John 1:7, 1:12, 1:50, 2:11, 2:22, 2:23, 2:24, **3:12, 3:15, 3:16, 3:18, 3:36,** 4:21, 4:39, 4:41, 4:42, 4:48, 4:50, 4:53, 5:24, 5:38, 5:44, 5:46, 5:47, 6:29,

6:30, 6:35, 6:36, 6:40, 6:47, 6:64, 6:69, 7:5, 7:31, 7:38, 7:39, 7:48, 8:24, 8:30, 8:31, 8:45, 8:46, 9:18, 9:35, 9:36, 9:38, 10:25, 10:26, 10:37, 10:38, 10:42, 11:15, 11:25, 11:26, 11:27, 11:40, 11:42, 11:45, 11:48, 12:11, 12:36, 12:37, 12:38, 12:39, 12:42, 12:44, 12:46, 12:47, 13:19, 14:1, 14:10, 14:11, 14:12, 14:29, 16:9, 16:27, 16:30, 16:31, 17:8, 17:20, 17:21, 19:35, 20:8, 20:25, 20:29, 20:31, Acts 2:44, 4:4, 4:32, 5:14, 8:12, 8:13, 8:37, 9:26, 9:42, 10:43, 11:17, 11:21, 13:12, 13:39, 13:41, 13:48, 14:1, 14:23, 15:5, 15:7, 15:11, 16:31, 16:34, 17:12, 17:34, 18:8, 18:27, 19:2, 19:4, 19:18, 21:20, 21:25, 22:19, 24:14, 26:27, 27:25, Romans 1:16, 3:2, 3:22, 4:3, 4:5, 4:11, 4:17, 4:18, 4:24, 6:8, 9:33, 10:4, 10:9, 10:10, 10:11, 10:14, 10:16, 13:11, 14:2, 15:13, 1 Corinthians 1:21, 3:5, 1 9:17, 11:18, 13:7, 14:22, 15:2, 15:11, 2 Corinthians 4:13, Galatians 2:7, 2:16, 3:6, 3:22, Ephesians 1:13, 1:19, Phil 1:29, 1 Thessalonians 1:7, 2:4, 2:10, 2:13, 4:14, 2 Thessalonians 1:10, 2:11, 2:12, 1 Timothy 1:11, 1:16, 3:16, 2 Timothy 1:12, Titus 1:3, s 3:8, Hebrews 4:3, 11:6, James 2:19, 2:23, 1 Peter 1:8, 1:21, 2:6, 2:7, 1 John 3:23, 4:1, 4:16, 5:1, 5:5, 5:10, 5:13, Jude 1:5, **Pistis** Matthew 8:10, 9:2, 9:22, 9:29, 15:28, 17:20, 21:21, 23:23, Mark 2:5, 4:40, 5:34, 10:52, 11:22, Luke 5:20, 7:9, 7:50, 8:25, 8:48, 17:5, 17:6, 17:19, 18:8, 18:42, 22:32, Acts 3:16, 6:5, 6:7, 6:8, 11:24, 13:8, 14:9, 14:22, 14:27, 15:9, 16:5, 17:31, 20:21, 24:24, 26:18, Romans 1:5, 1:8, 1:12, 1:17, 3:3, 3:22, 3:25, 3:26, 3:27, 3:28, 3:30, 3:31, 4:5, 4:9, 4:11, 4:12, 4:13, 4:14, 4:16, 4:19, 4:20, 5:1, 5:2, 9:30, 9:32, 10:6, 10:8, 10:17, 11:20, 12:3, 12:6, 14:1, 14:22, 14:23, 16:26, 1 Corinthians 2:5, 12:9, 13:2, 13:13, 15:14, 15:17, 16:13, 2 Corinthians 1:24, 4:13, 5:7, 8:7, 10:15, 13:5, Galatians 1:23, 2:16, 2:20, 3:2, 3:5, 3:7, 3:8, 3:9, 3:11, 3:12, 3:14, 3:22, 3:23, 3:24, 3:25, 3:26, 5:5, 5:6, 5:22, 6:10, Ephesians 1:15, 2:8, 3:12, 3:17, 4:5, 4:13, 6:16, 6:23, Phil 1:25, 1:27, 2:17, 3:9, Colossians 1:4, 1:23, 2:5, 2:7, 2:12, 1 Thessalonians 1:3, 1:8, 3:2, 3:5, 3:6, 3:7, 3:10, 5:8, 2 Thessalonians 1:3, 1:4, 1:11, 2:13, 3:2, 1 Timothy 1:2, 1:4, 1:5, 1:14, 1:19, 2:7, 2:15, 3:9, 3:13, 4:1, 4:6, 4:12, 5:8, 5:12, 6:10, 6:11, 6:12, 6:21, 2 Timothy 1:5, 1:13, 2:18, 2:22, 3:8, 3:10, 3:15, 4:7, Titus 1:1, 1:4, 1:13, 2:2, 2:10, 3:15, Phile 1:5, 1:6, Hebrews 4:2, 6:1, 6:12, 10:22 ,10:38, 10:39, 11:1, 11:3, 11:4, 11:5, 11:6, 11:7, 11:8, 11:9, 11:11 ,11:13, 11:17, 11:20, 11:21, 11:22, 11:23, 11:24, 11:27, 11:28, 11:29, 11:30, 11:31 ,11:33, 11:39, 12:2, 13:7, James 1:3, 1:6 ,2:1, 2:5, 2:14, 2:17, 2:18, 2:20, 2:22, 2:24, 2:26, 5:15, 1 Peter 1:5, 1:7,

1:9, 1:21, 5:9, 2 Peter 1:1 ,1:5, 1 John 5:4, Jude 1:3, 1:20, Revelation 2:13, 2:19,:10, 14:12.

Peitho (trust, persuaded, depend upon, set at ease, put confidence in, be convinced, certain, sure, follow, obey.)

Matthew 27:20, 27:43, 28:14, Mark 10:24, Luke 11:22, 16:31, 18:9, 20:6, Acts 5:36, 5:37, 5:40, 12:20, 13:43, 14:19, 17:4, 18:4, 19:8, 19:26, 21:14, 23:21, 26:26, 26:28, 27:11, 28:23, 28:24, Romans 2:8, 2:19, 8:38, 14:14, 15:14, 2 Corinthians 1:9, 2:3, 5:11, 10:7, Galatians 1:10, 3:1, **5:7, 5:10**, Phil 1:6, 1:14, 1:25, 2:24, 3:3, 3:4, 2 Thessalonians 3:4, 2 **Timothy 1:5, 1:12**, Phile 1:21, Hebrews 2:13, 6:9, 11:13, 13:17, 13:18, James 3:3, 1 **John 3:19.**

End Notes

1. Wells, David. *Losing Our Virtue: Why the Church Must Recover Its Moral Vision.* Wm. B. Eerdmans Publishing Co., Grand Rapids, MI, 1998, pages 127–128.
2. Keyes, Richard. *No God, But God: Breaking with the Idols of Our Age.* Ed. Os Guiness and John Seel, Moody Press, Chicago, IL, 1992, page 33.
3. Piper, Dr. John. *The Pleasures of God: Meditations on God's Delight in Being God.* Multnomah Publishing, Sister, OR, pages 215–216.
4. Edwards, Jonathan. *An Unpublished Essay on the Trinity.* monergism.com.
5. Peck, M. Scott, MD. *The Road Less Traveled and Beyond.* New York, NY, Touchstone Publishing, 1997, page 270.

CHAPTER SEVEN

Acceptance and Confidence

Harvard psychology professor Daniel Gilbert, in his bestselling book *Stumbling on Happiness*, describes how human beings are the only being (earthbound animal) with a highly developed frontal lobe as part of their brain. It seems that this part of the brain enables people to plan and project futures and how they feel about those futures that they imagine. The problem is more often than not we are wrong about the envisioning of those futures and how we will feel (how happy we will be) in those futures we envision. Gilbert writes, "The greatest achievement of the human brain is its ability to imagine objects and episodes that do not exist in the realm of the real, and it is this ability that allows us to think about the future. As one philosopher noted, the human brain is an 'anticipation machine' and 'making future' is the most important thing it does."[1]

Yet the problem is that our future imaginings are often flawed and outright wrong. Why do we look at things especially in this seemingly deceptive way? Gilbert says, "How do we manage to think of ourselves as great drivers, talented lovers, and brilliant chefs when the facts of our lives include a pathetic parade of dented cars, disappointed partners and deflated soufflés? The answer is simple: we cook the facts."[2]

Dr. Gilbert lays out four barriers to us humans having the ability to accurately imagine our future and especially barriers to accurately imagining how we will feel about the futures we imagine. The barriers are subjectivity, realism, presentism, and rationalization. So we imagine and plan for futures that we don't really want and imagine those futures making us happy when they won't. His remedy is very utilitarian, which is find someone who has the future we imagine and ask him or her how he or she feels. This, it seems to me, brings us right back to the very naiveté that Dr. Gilbert outlines in his book. "One person might be very happy in their life with a spouse, two children, a dog and a successful business venture and another person may be even more exceptionally fulfilled living in an area of immense need and caring for the needs of those around them without having all the amenities of others. In fact a case could be made that at any particular time either person described above may be intensely satisfied and at other times be intensely dissatisfied."[3]

Dr. Gilbert is right that we have a way of looking at things wrongly so that our choices are often misjudged and our planning for the future is very often wrongheaded. We have only our own subjective view; we need something, someone who can be unbiased, objective. We cannot discern the reality of what we imagine. There are holes in our imagining and we cannot imagine all of the contingencies that would add to or take away from our happiness by the future we imagine. Still again we fill in past emotional reactions to being in a certain situation with how we feel now about that situation. We tend to be overly nostalgic about the good old days, when as we were living the good old days we did not have quite the good feelings about that time that we hold in our memories. While at the same time we have a exceptional ability to rationalize to imagine things that we are predisposed to favorably and likewise things we have no objective experience with unfavorably.

James, the earthly half-brother of Jesus, Yeshua, Isa says; James 4:1–2: "What causes quarrels and what causes fights among you? Is it not this, that your passions are at war within you? You desire and do not have, so you murder. You covet and cannot obtain, so you fight and quarrel. You do not have, because you do not ask."

Os Guiness says, "If we were not marked by the results of the Fall, we would experience an unconscious natural harmony between our understanding, willing and feeling. All our actions and reactions would be whole. But none of us enjoy that perfect balance now, and alienation of sin means that we are alienated not only from God and each other but also from ourselves. The deep harmony within each of us has been lost. For some people, the alienation is so extreme that it leads to severe emotional disorder. For most of us the hassle of living with our contradictory 'selves' and struggling with our conflicting emotions, is a run-of-the-mill aspect of living. We are so used to putting up with the brokenness of our fallen human nature that we tend to accept it as normal and take it for granted."[4]

James 4:3: "You ask and do not receive, because you ask wrongly, to spend it on your passions."

Here is the real crux of our unhappiness: our passions are misplaced. We have a real inability to accept ourselves, and deep down we lack confidence in our choices. Sooner or later we come to the realization that we have been duped, or more likely we have duped ourselves; in looking for happiness, we have gone the wrong way. If we are honest, we can see that we are at odds with ourselves, weaving the wrong trail. The objective, absolute I AM, the three in one, is the only way to find our way to aligning our passions with what will truly bring happiness, where we will find the future we desire, the future we were made for.

I AM has been building that future for us. When the people of the Book had sunk to their lowest, they were again captives. They had built for themselves a future based on their own passions. This future had brought division, war, and exile. I AM came with a promise of His absolute love. Jeremiah 29:11-12: "For I know the plans I have for you, declares the LORD, plans for welfare and not for evil, to give you a future and a hope. Then you will call upon me and come and pray to me, and I will hear you."

Just as belief and trust come from looking away from self to looking at I AM, the three in one, acceptance of ourselves and confidence in ourselves runs through looking to I AM. To be made in the image of God is not intrinsic to us. It is intrinsic to I AM and the image is lost apart from I AM.

Ever since Eden our attempts to find fulfillment, to become who we really want to be, has been hampered by our own wrong sense of the future. Namely this is a future apart from I AM that brings death and destruction to our lives. The constant looking away to I AM is how we image forth the absolute image of God. This absolute love for us can most clearly be seen in Jesus, Isa, Yeshua. Colossians 1:15-20: "He is the image of the invisible God, the firstborn of all creation. For by him all things were created, in heaven and on earth, visible and invisible, whether thrones or dominions or rulers or authorities—all things were created through him and for him. And he is before all things, and in him all things hold together. And he is the head of the body, the church. He is the beginning, the firstborn from the dead, that in everything he might be preeminent. For in him all the fullness of God was pleased to dwell, and through him to reconcile to himself all things, whether on earth or in heaven, making peace by the blood of his cross."

I AM, the three in one, is the essence of acceptance and confidence. When Isaiah, Yeshua, Jesus began to teach and lead, He went to be baptized as a way to demonstrate humility, belief, and trust. When he was baptized, a voice from heaven that many people heard said (Matthew 3:16-17), "And when Jesus was baptized, immediately he went up from the water, and behold, the heavens were opened to him, and he saw the Spirit of God descending like a dove and coming to rest on him; and behold, a voice from heaven said, "This is my beloved Son, with whom I am well pleased."

Here all three of the one I AM stand forth in full acceptance of one another and confidence in one another. Millard Erickson writes, "The closeness of these three is accentuated through the fact that the goals, intentions, values, and objectives of each of the three is the same as those of each of the others ... There is also a closeness to the relationship due to the fact that each knows that there is no option of separation. Sometimes love among humans becomes tentative because there is the fear that the other will somehow turn away from the relationship or against the person himself/herself. This cannot be in the case of the three members of the Trinity, however. They are eternally and permanently one with the others."[5]

I AM, the three in one, is bathed in full acceptance and the confidence of that acceptance within Himself.

We cannot experience this level of acceptance outside of looking to I AM. Our plans for the future and future happiness are muddied in the mire of subjectivity, realism, presentism, and rationalization.

Writes Adrio Koenig, "The goal of the proclamation can be summed up as faith. As we proceed, it will become clear that much is contained in this one word ...

"We did not discuss personal faith ... when we spoke about the goal being realized 'for us.' There we saw that Christ achieved God's goal for us without our faith—indeed even before we were able to believe. Enmity was annihilated, peace restored, the new humanity created, the world redeemed, access to the Father obtained—all through Christ alone, without our faith ...

"But when the eschaton is attained in the second mode (i.e., in us), the call to faith is 'added' in quotation marks, for the moment, because it is not yet clear how anything could be added to the completeness of our salvation, justification, righteousness, peace, and access to the Father obtained by Jesus. Nevertheless, it is unmistakable that there is an addition, and that it is of decisive importance ...

"Before the proclamation's goal can be broadly outlined, it is necessary to show that this 'addition' of faith is no addition at all, and that because of the nature of faith there is agreement in reformation theology on the emptiness of faith. This does not mean that faith is unimportant, but rather that its importance—even indispensability—lies in that it is nothing on its own, is not autonomous, is no human contribution, but must receive its content and its meaning from the other side: in fact from God in Christ through the Spirit. In faith we confess God as the subject and ourselves as the object of salvation. Salvation means that Christ has fully attained God's goal for us. And when a person believes this, God's goal is attained in that person. Proclamation has as its goal to bring people to this knowledge and trust. How radically this faith involves our whole life is shown by the New Testament's equation of faith with obedience. So it is clear that by the nature of faith no tension can exist between 'Christ alone' and the 'addition' of faith. Faith lives solely from Christ, and is filled by what he has done. Stated in eschatological terms, Christ's attainment of the goal for us (but without us) and his attainment of the goal in us. Are not concurrent.

"Yet it is this very emptiness of faith in itself which leads to its decisive character. Because it is directed solely to Christ and his work for us, faith is necessary—and its lack excludes one from salvation. Without faith, God's goal in us is not reached. Precisely because faith is neither a human accomplishment nor a human contribution but rather a confession that everything has been done for us by Christ, we have no Christ if we have no faith. This is why Scripture speaks so strongly about the necessity, value, and power of faith. Faith receives value only from its object. And because of faith's necessity, we are bound to speak of the mortal peril of unbelief."[6]

Acceptance is the characteristic outgrowth of believing that gives us the ability to forgive ourselves and others so that healing and understanding can take place.

Confidence is the characteristic outgrowth of believing that gives us assurance of our being accepted and gives us the ability to look past self-promotion to the promotion of others so that their confidence is built up.

Given the fact that we so often make wrong choices and project for ourselves unhappy futures, it is no wonder that we often find it difficult to accept ourselves and lack confidence. Or confidence is misplaced in ourselves and we eventually find out, sometimes devastatingly, that our confidence was placed in someone who could not live up to that level of confidence. This is the real flaw in asking someone who is in the future that we imagine or plan for ourselves, that person may not as yet come to realization that he or she has put confidence in something that is ultimately unsatisfying.

Dietrich Bonhoeffer said, "Human love has little regard for truth. It makes the truth relative, since nothing, not even truth, must come between it and the beloved person. Human love desires the other person, his company, his answering love, but it does not serve him. On the contrary, it continues to desire even when it seems to be serving. There are two marks, both of which are one in the same thing, that manifest the difference between spiritual and human love: Human love cannot tolerate the dissolution of fellowship that has become false for the sake of genuine fellowship, and human love cannot love an enemy, that is, one who seriously and stubbornly resists it. Both spring from the same source: human love is by its very nature desire—desire for human community. So long as it can satisfy this desire in some way, it will not give it up, even for the sake of truth, even for the sake of genuine love to others. But where it can no longer expect its desire to be fulfilled, there it stops short—namely in the face of an enemy. There it turns to hatred, contempt and calumny.

"Right here is the point where spiritual love begins. This is why human love becomes personal hatred when it encounters genuine spiritual love, which does not desire but serves. Human love makes itself an end in itself. It creates of itself an end, an idol which it worships, to which it must subject everything. It nurses and cultivates an ideal, it loves itself, and nothing else in this world. Spiritual love, however, comes from Jesus Christ, it serves him alone; it knows that it has no immediate access to other persons.

"Jesus Christ stands between the lover and the others he loves. I do not know in advance what love to others means on the basis of the general idea of love that grows out of my human desires—all this may rather be hatred and an insidious kind of selfishness in the eyes of Christ. What love is, only Christ tells in his Word. Contrary to all my own opinions and convictions, Jesus Christ will tell me what love toward the brethren really is. Therefore, spiritual love is bound solely to the Word of Jesus Christ. Where Christ bids me to maintain fellowship for the sake of love, I will maintain it. Where his truth enjoins me to dissolve fellowship for love's sake, there I will dissolve it, despite all the protests of my human love. Because spiritual love does not desire but rather serves, it loves an enemy as a brother. It originates neither in the brother nor in the enemy but in Christ and his Word. Human love can never understand spiritual love, for spiritual love is from above; it is something completely strange, new, and incomprehensible to all earthly love.

"Because Christ stands between me and others, I dare not desire direct fellowship with them. As only Christ can speak to me in such a way that I may be saved, so others, too, can be saved only by Christ himself. This means that I must release the other person from every attempt of mine to regulate, coerce, and dominate him with my love. The other person needs to retain his independence of me; to be loved for what he is, as one for whom Christ became a man, died, rose again, for whom Christ brought forgiveness of sins and eternal life. Because Christ has long since acted decisively for my brother, before I could begin to act, I must leave him the freedom to be Christ's; I must meet him only as the person that he already is in Christ's eyes. This is the meaning of the proposition that we can meet others through the mediation of Christ. Human love constructs its own image of the other person, of what he is and what he should become. It takes the life of the other person into its own hands. Spiritual love recognizes the true image of the other person which he has received from Jesus Christ; the image that Jesus Christ himself embodied and would stamp upon all men.

"Therefore, spiritual love proves itself in that everything it says and does commends Christ. It will not seek to move others by all too personal, direct influence, by impure interference in the life of another. It will not take pleasure in pious, human fervor and excitement. It will rather meet the other person with the clear Word of God and be ready to leave him alone with this Word for a long time, willing to release him again in order that Christ may deal with him. It will respect the line that has been drawn between him and us by Christ, and it will find full fellowship with him in the Christ who alone binds us together. Thus this spiritual love will speak to Christ about a brother more than to a brother about Christ. It knows the most direct way to others is always through prayer to Christ and that love of others is wholly dependent upon truth in Christ. It is out of this love that John the disciple speaks. 'I have no greater joy than to hear that my children walk in truth' (3 John 4).

"Human love lives by uncontrolled and uncontrollable dark *desires*; spiritual love lives in the clear light of service ordered by *truth*. Human love produces human subjection, dependence, constraint; spiritual love creates *freedom* of the brethren under the Word. Human love breeds hothouse flowers; spiritual love creates the *fruits* that grow healthily in accord with God's good will in the rain and storm and sunshine of God's outdoors. The existence of any Christian life together depends on whether it succeeds at the right time in bringing out the ability to distinguish between a human ideal and God's reality, between spiritual and human community."[7]

Earlier we found out that what we do outwardly is really nothing, but the only thing that really matters is "faith working through love." Furthermore we found that there are only three things that remain ultimately in our lives: faith, hope, and love, and "the greatest of these is love." In the Book it is written (Hebrews 11:1), "Now faith is the assurance of things hoped for, the conviction of things not seen." Furthermore it says (Hebrews 11:6), "And without faith it is impossible to please him, for whoever would draw near to God must believe that he exists and that he rewards those who seek him."

What sets us as human beings apart from other creatures here on earth is our ability to plan and dream of the future. If we can accept and have confidence that what I AM will give us as reward for believing and trusting in Him is better than the future happiness we could imagine for ourselves, then we can truly accept and have confidence that He is absolute love. This will bring us a greater ability to accept and have confidence in others. We will not have our gaze focused on them, our faith in them, hope in future happiness fixed in them, but only fixed on I AM, absolute love. I AM says (Jeremiah 29:13), "You will seek me and find me, when you seek me with all your heart."

A. W. Tozer states, "From all this we learn that faith is not a once-done act, but a continuous gaze of the heart at the Triune God."[8]

Ratsah (acceptable, be pleased with, favorable to.)

Genesis 33:10, Leviticus 1:4, 7:18, 19:7, 22:23, 22:25, 22:27, 26:34, 26:41, 26:43, Deuteronomy 33:11 ,1 Samuel 29:4, 2 Samuel 24:23, 1 Chronicles 28:4, 29:3, 29:17, 2 Chronicles 10:7, 36:21, Esther 10:3, Job 14:6, 20:10, 34:9, Psalm 40:13, 50:18, **51:16**, 62:4, 102:14, 119:108, **147:10, 147:11**, 149:4, Proverbs 3:12, 16:7, Ecclesiastes 9:7, Isaiah 40:2, 42:1, Jeremiah 14:10, 14:12, Ezekiel 20:40, 20:41, 43:27, Hosea 8:13, Amos 5:22, Micah 6:7, Haggai 1:8, Malachi 1:8, 1:10, 1:13 **Ratson** Genesis 49:6, Exodus 28:38, Leviticus 1:3, 19:5, 22:19, 22:20, 22:21, 22:29, 23:11, Deuteronomy 33:16, 33:23, 33:24, 2 Chronicles 15:15 ,Ezra 10:11, Nehemiah 9:37, Esther 1:8, Psalm 5:12, 19:14, **30:5**, 30:7, 40:8, 51:18, 69:13, 89:17, 103:21, 106:4, 143:10, 145:16, 145:19, Proverbs 8:35, 10:32, 11:1, 11:20, 11:27, 12:2, ,12:22, 14:9, 14:35, 15:8, 16:13, 16:15, 18:22, 19:12, Isaiah 49:8, 56:7, 58:5, 60:7, 60:10, 61:2, Jeremiah 6:20, Daniel 8:4, 11:3, 11:16, 11:36, Malachi 2:13.

Kecel (confidence, loins, stupidity.)

Leviticus 3:4, 3:10, Leviticus 3:15, 4:9, 7:4, Job 8:14, 15:27, 31:24, Psalm 38:7, 49:13, **78:7,** Proverbs 3:26, Ecclesiastes 7:25. **Kiclah** Job 4:6, Psalm 85:8.

Proslambano (accept, take with, receive.)

Matthew 16:22, Mark 8:32, Acts 17:5, 18:26, 27:33, 27:34, 27:36, 28:2, **Romans 14:1, 14:3, 15:7** Phile 1:12, 1:17

Dechomai (approve, accept, take, receive.)

Matthew 10:14, 10:40, 11:14, 18:5, Mark 6:11, 9:37, 10:15, Luke 2:28, 8:13, 9:5, 9:11, 9:48, 9:53, 10:8, 10:10, 16:4, 16:6, 16:7, 16:9, 18:17, 22:17, John 4:45, Acts 3:21, 7:38, 7:59, 8:14, 11:1, 17:11, 21:17, 22:5, 28:21, **1 Corinthians 2:14**, 2 Corinthians 6:1, 7:15, 8:4, 8:17, 11:4, 11:16, Galatians

4:14, Ephesians 6:17, Phil 4:18, Colossians 4:10, 1 Thessalonians 1:6, 2:13, 2 **Thessalonians 2:10**, Hebrews 11:31, **James 1:21.**

Parrhesia (confidence, frankness, plainness of speech, courage, boldness, fearlessness, joyousness.)

Mark 8:32, John 7:4, 7:13, 7:26, 10:24, 11:14, 11:54, 16:25, 16:29, 18:20, Acts 4:13, 4:29, 4:31, 9:27, 28:31, 2 Corinthians 3:12, 7:4, **Ephesians 3:12, 6:**19, Phil 1:20, Colossians 2:15, 1 Timothy 3:13, , Phile 1:8, **Hebrews 3:6, 4:16, 10:19, 10:35, 1** John 2:28, 3:21, 4:17, 5:14

Pepoithesis (confidence, trust, faith.)

2 Corinthians 1:15, 3:4, 8:22, 10:2, Ephesians 3:12, Phil 3:4.

End Notes

1. Gilbert, Daniel. *Stumbling on Happiness*. Vintage Books, New York, NY, 2006, page 5.
2. Ibid., page 179.
3. Ibid
4. Guiness, Os. *God in the Dark*. Crossway Books, Wheaton, IL, 1996, page 127.
5. Erickson, Millard J. *God in Three Persons: A Contemporary Interpretation of the Trinity*. Baker Books, Grand Rapids, MI, 1995, page 226.
6. Koenig, Adrio. *The Eclipse of Christ in Eschatology: Toward a Christ Centered Approach*. Wm. B. Eerdmans Publishing, Grand Rapids, MI, 1989, pages 157-159. Adapted from Jesus die Laaste, Gelowig Nage Dink, Deel 2. Pretoria, DBC Bookshop, Marshall, Morgan and Scott, London, England, 1980.
7. Bonhoeffer, Dietrich. *Life Together: A Discussion of Christian Fellowship*. Harper and Row Publishers, Inc., 1954, pages 34-37. Published in Germany under Gemeinsames Leben.
8. Tozer, A. W. *The Pursuit of God*. Christian Publications, Inc., Harrisburg, PA, Tyndale House Publishers, Wheaton, IL, 1982-1983, page 90.

CHAPTER EIGHT

Gratitude and Compassion

The development and popularity of what has been identified as "positive psychology" has become an accepted form of the social sciences. "Positive psychology" focuses on the ways to improve the social and psychological health of individuals in order to increase productivity and happiness. In fact, most of the research involves an attempt to discover in what manner true complete or persistent happiness may be developed.

Psychologists have come to discover that human beings have a bent toward, we might say *a natural disposition* toward, the bad or negative. In an article in *American Psychologist* (November 2006), Martin E. P. Seligman, Tayyab Rashid, and Acacia C. Parks of the Positive Psychology Center at the University of Pennsylvania write, "The negative quite easily attract human attention and memory, and the larger literature on "bad is stronger than good" (Baumeister, Bratlavsky, Finkenauer, & Vohs, 2001) testifies to this. It makes evolutionary sense that negative emotions, tied as they are to threat, loss and trespass, should trump happiness."[1]

It is a wonder here again that the scientific bias toward attributing a disposition that is naturally intent on the bad and negative to natural selection, as opposed to the fall of mankind in the garden where threat, loss and trespass ruined happiness. However, the authors continue: "Human beings are naturally biased to remembering the negative, attending to the negative, and expecting the worst."[2] It is this tendency that is the inevitable cause of unhappiness, depression, and the progression to other psychological and physical maladies, leading further to disease and psychosis.

The connection between our current inescapable disposition toward, might I say *cursedness*, is a barrier to our inability to lasting happiness (blessedness), or I might say *everlasting happiness*. People of the Book might well remember the words of the law giver Moses in Deuteronomy 30:15-20: "See, I have set before you today life and good, death and evil. "If you obey the commandments of the LORD your God that I command you today, by loving the LORD your God, by walking in his ways, and by keeping his commandments and his statutes and his rules, then you shall live and multiply, and the LORD your God will bless you in the land that you are entering to take possession of it. But if your heart turns away, and you will not hear, but are drawn away to worship other gods and serve them, I declare to you today, that you shall surely perish. You shall not live long in the land that you are going over the Jordan to enter and possess. I call heaven and earth to witness against you today, that I have set before you life and death, blessing and curse. Therefore choose life, that you and your offspring may live, loving the LORD your God, obeying his voice and holding fast to him, for he is your life and length of days."

Positive psychology though has discovered an antidote to our predicament; psychologists have discovered that there are three paths or environments for happiness. The three paths are seemingly integrated, progressive, and cumulative. The first path is "the Pleasant Life." It consists of pleasures or the more hedonic emotions associated with pleasures. These emotions, brought on by pleasurable activities, produce positive feelings about the future and build hope, faith, trust, and confidence. The happiness elicited by "the Pleasant Life" also includes positive emotions about the past including satisfaction, contentment, fulfillment, and serenity. A second path or level of happiness is "the Engaged Life" where happiness is experienced through strong engagements with life that pursues involvement and absorption with others and the world around us. The main idea is a focus beyond oneself where it is said "the self is lost."

A third path and level of happiness is "the Meaningful Life" involving the pursuit of meaning. At the level of "the Meaningful Life," the authors say, "This consists in using one's signature strengths and talents to belong and serve something that one believes is bigger than self. It is then as all three of these paths convene and fully intertwine that we find "the Full Life."

The research concludes that it is really only activities that help individuals to focus on "meaning" and "engagement" to be significantly impactful and correlated highly to a higher level of life satisfaction and a lower incidence of depression. The center of the therapeutic interventions for moving toward "the Full Life" focus on three highly impactful areas: gratitude and forgiveness training, optimism and hope, love and attachment.[3]

In another paper published in the *Journal of International Association of Applied Psychology* in 2008, Martin E. P. Seligman outlines physical and psycho-social benefits of positive psychology. Effects were cited for positive results of positive affect in protection against disease, such as coronary and cardiovascular events, stroke, depression, frailty measurements, hospitalization recovery time was seen to be reduced and even colds and influenza were seen as reduced. Many psychologists see gratitude and gratitude intervention as one of the most helpful and positive affective treatments for psychological health.[4]

Alex Wood, Stephen Joseph, and Alex Liney write in *The Psychologist* (January 2007) an article titled "Gratitude: Parent of All Virtues." In it, they say, "The first reason that gratitude may be an important personality trait is because it seems to have one of the strongest links with mental health of any personality variable."[3]

Lawrence J. Crabb Jr. and Daniel B. Allender have written the following:

> It is a mistake to think of encouragement as a set of specific words or phrases. Encouragement depends less on which words we use than on the motivation behind them. Words that encourage are (1) inspired by love, and (2) directed toward fear. These two conditions must

be met for words to encourage. Let us look at these conditions in more detail.

Condition 1: Words that encourage are prompted by love, not by fear; that is, the words spoken must never function as a layer for the speaker;   .

Condition 2: Words that encourage are aimed not at another's layers with the intent of rearranging them, but rather at another's hidden fear with the intent of reducing it ...

To be encouraging, words must be prompted by love. That's the first condition. The second condition is equally important: they must be directed to fear. From my love to another's fear—that's the formula. Words of rebuke, exhortation, suggestion, instruction, or sympathy must all meet these two conditions if they are to further God's purposes and qualify as words of encouragement.

Targeting our words toward fear of another is an easily stated but often misunderstood concept. Too many people reason like this: "All this encouragement business about warmth and supportiveness and acceptance is really off the mark. It fails to address the real problem and evidences a weak view of sin. People need less affirmation and more exhortation to put off the old man and put on the new."

People with "executive personalities" (who rarely have close friends) mercilessly pound others about their responsibilities. They apply pressure in every available way to compel others to have devotions, witness, attend church, and tithe. Some people, depending on their temperament, conform to the pressure and appear to move along nicely on the road to spiritual maturity. Others rebel. In either case, little heart movement toward God takes place.

The still popular cult of Christian self-love, whose cardinal teaching is "You must learn to love yourself," leads to the reaction to harsh exhorters by swinging to the other extreme. "We just need to be warm and unconditionally caring. Exhortation, calls to discipline, and pressure to make commitments are all counterproductive to spiritual growth. People need an atmosphere of loving acceptance for growth to occur. Only in the context of love will personal maturity develop."

These people come dangerously close to buying into humanism, an unbiblical philosophy that affirms the inherent goodness of man and argues that problems result when society thwarts the expression of that goodness by an oppressive system of laws and sanctions. Christians need to divorce themselves from this idea by recognizing the radical results of mankind's fall into sin. The truth is, people have no natural tendency to conform their lives to the character of God. Straying from the path of righteousness is as natural to us as bucking is to a bronco.

Spiritual regeneration by the Holy Spirit provides us with new motivation and goals, but our sinful tendencies remain. Therefore we do require exhortation, rebuke discipline— and the Bible is filled with it. The prophet Amos would have scorned the notion that Jews of his day were essentially cooperative people needing only a loving environment for their real selves to blossom with love and good deeds. The Bible instructs us to "stimulate" each other to greater love and better behavior (Hebrews. 10:24). Passively accepting people where they are until they get around to godly living is not a biblical strategy for encouragement.

Encouragement, therefore, must not be defined as either rigorous exhortation or accepting warmth. Both will be involved in the work of encouragement, but neither gets at the essence of what encouragement is. Encouragement depends on loving motivation in the encourager as well as wisdom to discern the needs of the person accurately. The actual words used may be admonishing, rebuking, correcting, reproving, instructing, explaining, sympathizing, reflecting, affirming or self-disclosing. If the motive is love and the target is fear, the words will be encouraging."[6]

Against these, there is no need for laws; love, joy, peace, patience, kindness, goodness, faithfulness, gentleness, and self-control Galatians 5:22-23. Of course this is not a new declaration; it is the outworking of I AM, the three in one, through the personal life of the Spirit of I AM, the three in one, as we look to Him.

As scientific data is gathered and analyzed, it is clear how much I AM, the three in one, and His Word to us is vindicated and verified. It is also true that the presuppositions we bring to scientific proofs will seem to verify our conclusions whether naturally developed or divinely initiated and governed.

J. I. Packer and Thomas Howard say, "The question of esteem and identity now appear in a new light. What the psychologists and gurus offered us was self-discovery through introspection, self-scrutiny, and self-love. What Christ in the gospel offers us is, in effect, self-discovery through self-abandonment to God's love. This is self-discovery not in isolation, but in relationship; not by shutting oneself up to keep the world out and withdrawing in to some inner sanctum of the psyche, but by opening oneself up to the invading Savior and letting him lead one's heart out into the world in sympathetic care and concern for others. The esteem which creates and shapes our identity, and thereby leads us to a strong and joyful sense of identity, is the redeeming love of our creator to us his sinful creatures. We deserve to be shaken off into hell, as one shakes an insect off one's hand into the fire, and here is God seeking to love us into heaven at the cost of the death of his Son. And the gospel affirms that all avenues to self-discovery apart from opening myself to God's approach are blind alleys, for the notion of myself to which they lead me, however agreeable, consoling, bracing, and fascinating it may be(and what can be more fascinating to sinners than the study of themselves?) is precisely not "me," any more than the notion of myself which by its collapse sent me flying to the shrinks and gurus was 'me.' In telling me how I function in terms of my make-up the counselors are *not* telling me who I am; that is something which only God makes known to me. There is no way in heaven, earth or hell that I know myself without knowing the One who made me, and for whom I was made in the first instance, and from whom I should never have lapsed.

"But there is more to the matter of my identity than just this. From Jesus Christ I receive a new identity, which is henceforth my true identity as a sinner now redeemed, an identity which I may truly know as the real "me." This new identity has two aspects, just as my natural identity does: namely, the relational and the dispositional. The relational aspect has to do with commitment and identification. As Christian marriage changes a woman's identity, because she commits herself to her husband as leader and identifies with the task of furthering his welfare and his interests, so Christian faith changes the believers identity; for having committed myself to follow Christ. I am now bidden to identify myself with him in such a way that the pattern of his life, death, and resurrection become the pattern of my own existence henceforth. His laying aside of his prerogatives, rights, dignities, and interests, here on earth and his laying down of his life for others must be reproduced in me here and now at the level of motives, goals and strategies. I am, in short, to imitate Christ, to model myself on him, to walk as he walked, indeed to *be* Christ in my attitudes to other people.

The dispositional aspect of our new identity springs from the reality of our new creation. People who become Christians may look the same from the outside as they did before, but they are not the same inside. They are new people, radically altered—though they themselves may not fully at first appreciate this. Deep down within them, however, deeper than depth psychology can plumb or sustained introspection can reach, God has changed the motivational core of their personality—what Scripture calls the "heart"—in such a way that now there moves within them a longing and love for God: God's will, God's truth, God's service, God's fellowship, God's honor and glory. It is a desire to know and please and enjoy and share the God of one's salvation, and only as this desire is satisfied is their heart at all contented. So, whereas before it was one's nature to live to oneself, it is now what may almost be called and instinctual drive to live for God, and worship becomes the deepest joy of one's heart."[7]

I AM, the three in one, *is* the happiest being of all. He does whatever He pleases. Psalm 135:6-7: "Whatever the LORD pleases, he does, in heaven and on earth, in the seas and all deeps. He it is who makes the clouds rise at the end of the earth, who makes lightnings for the rain and brings forth the wind from his storehouses."

In His abundant uncontained happiness He overflows with absolute love to people. He has no needs because everything belongs to Him and was created by Him. If a need would arise, He would create the satisfier of the need. His love to us overflows out of the absolute love within Himself.

Deuteronomy 10:14-15: "Behold, to the LORD your God belong heaven and the heaven of heavens, the earth with all that is in it. Yet the LORD set his heart in love on your fathers and chose their offspring after them, you above all peoples, as you are this day."

The absolute love of I AM, the three in one, flows from the Father to the Son and the Son to the Father and is transmitted between the three by the Spirit. Each person within the one has a distinct role in the overflowing love that comes to us as we are established by love to hope in Him. Psalm 147:10–11: "His delight is not in the strength of the horse, nor his pleasure in the legs of a man, but the LORD takes pleasure in those who fear him, in those who hope in his steadfast love."

His personal delight, His gratitude, is reflected in the activity of His Son Jesus, Yeshua, Isa. Matthew 17:1–5: "And after six days Jesus took with him Peter and James, and John his brother, and led them up a high mountain by themselves. And he was transfigured before them, and his face shone like the sun, and his clothes became white as light. And behold, there appeared to them Moses and Elijah, talking with him. And Peter said to Jesus, 'Lord, it is good that we are here. If you wish, I will make three tents here, one for you and one for Moses and one for Elijah.' He was still speaking when, behold, a bright cloud overshadowed them, and a voice from the cloud said, 'This is my beloved Son, with whom I am well pleased; listen to him.'"

The happy gratitude of I AM that flows out of the relational absolute love of I AM is evident. God eternally enjoys the relationship of the three. Absolute love flows out in compassion toward His creation. His overflowing compassionate love allows Him to be slow to anger and to forgive thousands to overflow with steadfast love. I AM needs no gratitude or forgiveness therapy. It is the core of His existence; it is His Glory revealed.

Gratitude is the characteristic outgrowth of believing that gives us the ability to look at all good things as gifts from God and causes us to give in return so the gifts can be shared by all. Compassion is the characteristic outgrowth of believing that gives us the ability to be gracious (giving undeserved favor) and merciful (not demanding retribution) so that we might live in a way that will be most beneficial to ourselves and others and glorifying to God.

The irony of much thinking about man is that the elimination of a creator makes the creature think more highly of self than we ought to think, putting ourselves into the place where we believe by our own mechanistic, social, and psychological designs we can make the kind of world we desire; that we believe will make us happy. The studies indicated that, at the longest, the positive results of the gratitude and forgiveness therapy lasted only about six months. On the other hand, we throw away any hope of lasting happiness or everlasting happiness by not having an absolute mooring from which happiness is imparted.

Francis A. Schaeffer writes, "One of the problems with humanists is that they tend to 'love' humanity as whole—Man with a capital M, Man as an idea—but forget about man as an individual, as a person. Christianity is to be the exact opposite. Christianity is not to love in abstraction, but to love the individual who stands before me in a person to person relationship. He must never be faceless to me or I am denying everything I say I believe. This concept will always involve some cost: it is no cheap thing, because we live in a fallen world, and we ourselves are fallen.

"Now we must ask, what happens when someone has been hurt by my sin? The Bible teaches that the moment we have confessed this sin to God, the shed blood of Jesus is enough to cleanse the moral guilt. As Christians we insist that all sin is ultimately against God. When I hurt the man, I sin against God. But let us never forget that this does not change the fact that because man has been made in the image of God, the man I have hurt has real value. And this must be important to me, not only as a concept but in my practice and demonstration. My fellowman is not unimportant: he is God's image-bearer. That is true of the non-Christian man as well as of the Christian. He is lost, but he is still a man. Thus when God says, 'My child, this sin is different; in this sin you have hurt another person.' I respond, 'What shall I do LORD?' And the answer is clear from the Word of God: 'Make it right with the man you have hurt. The man you have hurt is not a zero.'

"But what is the usual reaction when God says to me, 'Go make it right'? It is to answer, 'But that would be humiliating.' Yet surely, if I have been willing to tell God I am sorry when I have sinned, I must be willing to tell this to the man I have hurt. How can I say, 'I am sorry' to God, if I am not willing to say, 'I am sorry' to the man I have hurt, when he is my equal, my fellow creature, my kind? Such repentance is meaningless hypocrisy. We cannot just trample human relationships and expect our relationship to God to be lovely, beautiful and open. This is not only a matter of what is legally right, but of a true relationship of person to person on the basis of who I am and who the man is.

"In James 5:16 we are told, 'Confess your faults one to another.' We are not told to confess our faults to a priest, nor to the group, unless the group has been harmed, but to the person we have harmed. This is a very simple admonition, but in our present imperfect state, very difficult to obey. To go and say, 'I am sorry' is to enter by the low door; first in confessing to God, and then to the individual harmed. Let me emphasize, this is a *person* before me, a human being, made in God's image. So it is not such a low door after all, all it involves is being willing to admit our equality with the one we have hurt. Being his equal it is perfectly right that I should want to say, 'I am sorry.' Only a desire to be superior makes me afraid to confess and apologize.

"If I am in living relationship with the Trinity, my human relationships become more important in one way, because I see the real value of man, but less important in another way because I do not need to be God in these relationships any longer. So now I can go up to the man and say, 'I am sorry for such and such a specific harm I have done you,' without smashing the integration point of my universe, because it is no longer myself, but God."[8]

Acknowledging, loving, worshipping a creator, and realizing ourselves as being created allow us as creatures to think rightly about ourselves and become happy, everlastingly happy only as we everlastingly keep our focus upon I AM, the three in one, from whom happiness overflows; gratitude is constantly exuded and forgiveness is poured out.

Yadah (gratitude, throw, cast, confess, give thanks, praise, laud.) Genesis 29:35, 49:8, Leviticus 5:5, 16:21, 26:40, Numbers 5:7, 2 **Samuel 22:50,** 1 Kings 8:33, 8:35, 1 **Chronicles 16:4, 16:7, 16:8, 16:34, 16:35, 16:41,** 23:30, 25:3, 29:13, 2 Chronicles 5:13, 6:24, 6:26, 7:3, 7:6, 20:21, 30:22, 31:2, Ezra 3:11 ,10:1, Nehemiah 1:6, 9:2, 9:3, 11:17, 12:24, 12:46, Job 40:14, Psalm 6:5, 7:17, 9:1 ,18:49, 28:7, 30:4, 30:9, 30:12, 32:5, 33:2, 35:18, 42:5, 42:11, 43:4, 43:5, 44:8, 45:17, 49:18, 52:9, 54**:6,** 57:9, 67:3, 67:5, 71:22, 75:1, 76:10, 79:13, 86:12, 88:10, 89:5, 92:1, 97:12, 99:3, **100:4,** 105:1 ,106:1,

106:47, **107:1, 107:8, 107:15, 107:21 ,107:31** ,108:3, 109:30, 111:1, 118:1 ,118:19, 118:21, 118:28, 118:29, 119:7, 119:62, 122:4, 136:1 ,136:2, 136:3, 136:26, 138:1 ,138:2, 138:4, 139:14, 140:13, 142:7, 145:10, Proverbs 28:13, Isaiah 12:1 ,12:4, 25:1, 38:18, 38:19, Jeremiah 33:11, 50:14, Lamentations 3:53, **Daniel 9:4, 9:20**, Zechariah 1:21.

Rakam (compassion, love.) Genesis 43:14, 49:25, Exodus 33:19, Leviticus 11:18, Deuteronomy 13:17, 14:17, 30:3, Judges 5:30, 2 Samuel 24:14, 1 Kings 8:50, 2 Kings 13:23, 1 Chronicles 2:44, 21:13, 2 **Chronicles 30:9**, Nehemiah 1:11 ,9:19, 9:27, 9:28, 9:31, Psalm 18:1, 25:6, **40:11, 51:1, 69:16,** 77:9, 79:8, 102:13, **103:4, 103:13**, 106:46, **116:5,** 119:77, 119:156, 145:9, Proverbs 12:10, 28:13, 30:16, Isaiah 9:17, 13:18, 14:1, 27:11, **30:18,** 46:3, 47:6, 49:10, 49:13, 49:15, **54:7, 54:8, 54:10, 55:7, 60:**10, 63:7, 63:15, Jeremiah 6:23, 12:15, 13:14, 16:5, 21:7, 30:18, 31:20, 33:26, 42:12, 50:42, **Lamentations 3:22, 3:32**, Ezekiel 20:26, 39:25, Daniel 9:9, 9:18, Hosea 1:6, 1:7, 2:1, 2:4, 2:19, 2:23, 14:3, Amos 1:11, Micah 7:19, Habakkuk 3:2, Zechariah 1:12, 1:16, 7:9, 10:6 **Rakum** (compassion, softness, gentleness.) **Exodus 34:6**, Deuteronomy 4:31, 2 Chronicles 30:9, Nehemiah 9:17, 9:31, Psalm 78:38, 86:15, 103:8, 111:4, 112:4, 145:8, **Joel 2:13, Jonah 4:2.**

Eucharistia (gratitude, thankfulness.) Acts 24:3, 1 Corinthians 14:16, 2 Corinthians 4:15, 9:11, 9:12, Ephesians 5:4, Phil 4:6, Colossians 2:7, 4:2, 1 Thessalonians 3:9, 1 Timothy 2:1, **4:3, 4:4**, Revelation 4:9, 7:12 **Eucharisteo** (be thankful, feel obligated, give or return thanks) Matthew 15:36, 26:27, Mark 8:6, 14:23, Luke 17:16, 18:11, 22:17, 22:19, John 6:11, 6:23, 11:41, Acts 27:35, 28:15, **Romans 1:8, 1:21,** 7:25, 14:6, 16:4, 1 Corinthians 1:4, 1:14, 10:30, 11:24, 14:17, 14:18, 2 Corinthians 1:11, Ephesians 1:16, 5:20, Phil 1:3, **Colossians 1:3, 1:12, 3:17, 1** Thessalonians 1:2, 2:13, 5:18, 2 Thessalonians 1:3, 2:13, Phile 1:4, Revelation 11:17.

Eleos (compassion, mercy, pity.) **Matthew 9:13, 12:7, 23:23,** Luke 1:50, 1:54, 1:58, 1:72, 1:78, **10:37,** Romans 9:23, 11:31 ,15:9, Galatians 6:16 ,**Ephesians 2:4, 1** Timothy 1:2, 2 Timothy 1:2, 1:16, 1:18, Titus 1:4, **3:5,** Hebrews 4:16, **James 2:13, 3:17, 1** Peter 1:3, 2 John 1:3, Jude 1:2, 1:21.

End Notes

1. Seligman, Martin E. P.; Rashid, Tayyab; and Parks, Acacia C. *American Psychologist.* November 2006.
2. Ibid.
3. Ibid.
4. Seligman, Martin E. P. *Journal of International Association of Applied Psychology.* 2008.
5. Wood, Alex; Joseph, Stephen; and Liney, Alex. *The Psychologist.* January 2007.
6. Crabb, Lawrence J. and Allender, Daniel B. *Encouragement the Key to Caring.* Pyranee Books, Zondervan Publishing House, Grand Rapids, MI, 1984, pages 71-79.
7. Packer, J. I. and Howard, Thomas. *Christianity: The True Humanism.* Word Inc., Waco, TX, 1985, pages 233-234.
8. Schaeffer, Francis A. *True Spirituality.* Tyndale House Publishers, Wheaton, IL, 1971, pages 157, 158.

CHAPTER NINE

Freedom, Stewardship, and Servanthood

The United States of America's Declaration of Independence is a definitive cry against tyrannical rule that limits the very nature of being humans. The famous words "We hold these truths to be self-evident, that all men are created equal that they are endowed by their Creator with certain unalienable Rights, that among these are Life, Liberty and the pursuit of Happiness." The words to follow may be known or at least noted less: "That to secure these rights, Governments are instituted among Men, deriving their just powers from the consent of the governed, —That whenever any Form of Government becomes destructive of these ends, it is the Right of the People to alter or to abolish it, and to institute new Government, laying its foundation on such principles and organizing its powers in such form, as to them shall seem most likely to effect their Safety and Happiness. Prudence, indeed, will dictate that Governments long established should not be changed for light and transient causes; and accordingly all experience hath shewn, that mankind are more disposed to suffer, while evils are sufferable, than to right themselves by abolishing the forms to which they are accustomed. But when a long train of abuses and usurpations, pursuing invariably the same Object evinces a design to reduce them under absolute Despotism, it is their right, it is their duty, to throw off such Government, and to provide new Guards for their future security."

Tyrannical governments and despotic rulers, whether under the name of a so-called "god" or to make themselves to be god, are the wasteland of human history. The carnage flows back to the fall and our eviction from standing in the presence of I AM, the three in one. The loss of life, liberty, and everlasting happiness is inevitably the result of separation from Him. Thinking that I AM might be withholding some pleasure or benefit from us, we seek to find benefit elsewhere. In seeking freedom from the creator, the creature has become trapped in the prisons of our own making. There is no absolute apart from Him. The inalienable rights of life, liberty, and the pursuit of happiness being self-evident also evidence the purpose of I AM in the way He created the world.

Consider the words of Daniel Fuller: "In looking back over redemptive history, therefore, it should be plain that the earth will render proper worship to God not only to the extent that it is filled with those who worship him but also to the extent of the zeal with which they worship him. Had it not been vital for God to order holy history so that later generations would worship him the more fervently, it is conceivable that there would have been no need for a redemptive history that consists in an extended overlap between this evil age and the glorious age to come. However, we know that God's own intense love for his glory cannot settle for anything less from the world he has created, for Jesus said that he would spit out of his mouth those who had mere lukewarm love for him (Revelation 3:16). Therefore God ordained a redemptive history whose sequence fully displays his glory so that, at the end, the greatest possible number of people would have had the historical antecedent necessary to engender fervent love for God. Thus Paul sums it all up in Romans 11:32: "God has bound all men over to disobedience so that he may have mercy on them all." Viewing redemptive history in this light then evokes in Paul the doxology of verses 33–36.

"But some might ask, Why does God not use his omnipotence to make everyone sing such a doxology from the start and thus avoid the extended overlap and the problem of evil that redemptive history entails? The answer is that God could find no delight in a creation that, puppet-like, was forced to love him. His love for himself arises freely, that is, because he sees clearly that he is indeed worthy of all his own worship. And unless creation's delight in God is also a free act, arising from the full display of all his glory in the sequence of redemptive history, creation would not be consonant with God's delight in himself, and God could not tolerate it.

"The one thing, therefore, that God is doing in all of redemptive history is to show forth his mercy in such a way that the greatest number of people will throughout eternity delight in him with all their heart, strength, and mind. When the earth of the new creation is filled with such people, then God's purpose in showing forth his mercy will have been achieved. The "glorious freedom" (Romans 8:21) that will then be enjoyed by the children of God and the complete orderliness of all creation, in contrast to the 'frustration' that now prevails (v. 20), will represent the fullness of God's glory by showing that he was so sufficient in himself that he could find complete fulfillment and blessedness simply in mercifully imparting the ultimate blessing to creation, with no ulterior purpose beyond that. All the events of redemptive history and their meaning as recorded in the Bible compose a unity in that they conjoin to bring about this goal."[1]

The clear evidence of mankind is that we have chosen a liberty, freedom from I AM's absolute love, to find ourselves imprisoned by our own limitedness. We are the creatures and I AM is the creator. We are finite in resource and I AM is infinite in resource. We are vulnerable and prone to error, I AM is invulnerable and the one who establishes truth. Human history is a history of futility in finding liberty, of destroying life of heartache and immense toil in the pursuit of happiness. What did I AM say? "You will surely die." The promise of increased pain, toil, sweat, thorns, thistles, and loss of freedom and happiness are a reality and all of us return to the dust from which we were formed.

If, as has been said, "the chief end of man is to glorify God and enjoy Him forever," we have gone astray from that exponentially. Freedom, true liberty, is found in becoming what we were meant to be as creatures. As I have said, it is ironic that the more we realize our place as creatures before a creator the more we are likely to hold up one another as significant and unique, valued. We are equal in place as creatures but distinct in role, and I AM has created each of us to be everlastingly happy as that role is fulfilled by us and in us.

J. I. Packer writes in contrasting the world's idea of freedom as absence of restraint with the Bible's idea of freedom: "The second approach to freedom is distinctly Christian. It is evangelical, personal and positive. It defines freedom persuasively, that is, in terms which (so it urges) all should recognize as expressing what they are really after. The terms relate not to externals, which vary from age to age and person to person, but to unchanging realities of the inner life. This definition starts with freedom from and freedom not to—in this case, freedom from the guilt and power of sin, and freedom not to be dominated by tyrannical self will—but it centers on freedom for: freedom for God and godliness, freedom to love and serve one's Maker and fellow creatures, freedom for the joy, hope and contentment which God gives to sinners who believe in Christ. The essence of freedom (so the claim runs) lies in these inward qualities of the heart, of which modern secular man knows nothing.

"This approach sees freedom as an inner state of all who are fulfilling the potential of their own created nature by worshipping and serving their Savior—God from the heart. Their freedom is freedom not to do wrong, but to do right; not to break the moral law, but to keep it, not to forget God, but to cleave to him every moment, in every endeavor and relationship; not to abuse and exploit others, but to lay down one's life for them(cf. John 15:12, 13; 1 John 3:16). Freedom for such free service and self giving is beyond the capacity, even the comprehension, of fallen human nature. At first sight few can recognize it as freedom at all. Though it is really the way of life for which we were made, it so negates the self-absorbed lifestyle which we all instinctively choose that it seems to us anti-human and frightens us off. In fact, the only way anyone comes to know it at all is as a gift of the risen Christ, who affirms his penitent disciples in their self-denial and imparts his life to us as we give away our own.

"One aspect of this freedom is integrity that simplicity and purity of heart which, as Kierkegaard analyzed it, consists in willing one thing, namely the will and glory of God, so that one's motives are freed from the taint of self regard. A second aspect is spontaneity. Unlike the rule-ridden Pharisees, whom Jesus pictured living (as it were) by numbers, the free person in Christ invests creative enterprise and resourcefulness in the task of pleasing and praising God and doing good to one's fellows. Where Pharisees concern is simply to avoid doing wrong, the free person seeks to make the most and best of every situation, thus becoming lively and sometimes breathtaking company. A final aspect is contentment, the fruit of God's gift of a joy within that increases all life's pleasures, stays with one whatever is present or lacking in one's outward circumstances, and enables one to accept without bitterness the most acute forms of suffering and pain. In short, the real Christian—for that is the person I am describing—is free for holiness, humanness and happiness—a freedom which surely merits its name."[2]

Now this is a twist on freedom: not being free to do anything at all, being free to become exactly what we were created for, glorifying I AM. We were each of us born to uniquely image forth I AM. It will take an infinite number of us infinitely with individual roles to image forth what is infinite. In order to realize this kind of freedom, we must be captivated by I AM, the three in one. It is only through being willingly captivated and passionately enamored by the infinite I AM, who is absolute love, that we can fully find freedom to be what through us fully reflects back to Him what will make us everlastingly happy. This freedom only comes from being willingly captive to I AM, the three in one, who is the only absolutely free being, uncreated, eternal, all knowing, all wise, all loving, all powerful, without beginning or end, and unchangeable. We can only say along with Paul who was miraculously changed from a despotic, murdering religious bigot to find happiness in being captivated by I AM. Romans 11:29-36: "For the gifts and the calling of God are irrevocable. For just as you were at one time disobedient to God but now have received mercy because of their disobedience, so they too have now been disobedient in order that by the mercy shown to you they also may now receive mercy. For God has consigned all to disobedience, that he may have mercy on all. Oh, the depth of the riches and wisdom and knowledge of God! How unsearchable are his judgments and how inscrutable his ways! 'For who has known the mind of the Lord, or who has been his counselor?' 'Or who has given a gift to him that he might be repaid?' For from him and through him and to him are all things. To him be glory forever. Amen."

So also the history of mankind is the history of I AM, the three in one, coming again and again to show mercy, pour out grace, and bring freedom to anyone who will have it.

Freedom requires constraints and in an environment of separateness from absolute love it requires restraints. I AM, the three in one, is constrained by absolute love. He is absolutely self controlled. There are no controls outside of the being of I AM that could restrain Him. He is slow to anger. He forestalls His anger in the face of rebellious creatures. The fruit of looking only to I AM, three in one, includes self-control. 2 Corinthians 5:14: "For the love of Christ controls us, because we have concluded this: that one has died for all, therefore all have died." 2 Corinthians 5:15: "And he died for all, that those who live might no longer live for themselves but for him who for their sake died and was raised."

The love of I AM controls, or elsewhere it says constrains, us apart from this love are needed restraints. Then it must be clear that we are not absolutely free, we do not have that capacity, and we are not all knowing or all powerful. We are only free in full, perfected relationship to I AM.

Richard Lovelace says, "Patients tested for glaucoma are shown a circle which represents their visual field and then asked to point out the areas they can see. The disease typically darkens the center of the field, while leaving some vision on the periphery. The fallen mind's view of the world is like that of a glaucoma patient. Its view of all things is darkened and distorted by sin, but it has sort of twilight vision of the periphery of life. In the inner circle of ultimate concerns, however, it is in deeper darkness. It has at best only a dim apprehension of the grandeur of God, the depth of its own need, and the real significance of its relationship to other people.

"The gift of faith is a divine healing of this central blindness of the soul. It is an exact reversal of the entrance into darkness which was the essence of the Fall. Through faith in the Messiah, the soul is able to face reality again with cleared vision. As T. S. Elliot said, 'Humankind cannot bear very much reality.' But through the light shed by the Holy Spirit on the Messiah and his saving work, the soul can take in at a glance the truth about its own standing before God. It can bear the bad news about the justice of God and the depth of its sin, because it can see in the same glance the good news of the grace of Christ available simply through faith.

"The blaze of this illumination, faith necessarily involves repentance. The Greek word for repentance, metanoia, literally means "a change of mind" toward God, toward oneself and toward others. It is a Copernican revolution in which the self is evicted from the center of life, and the Messiah is enthroned instead. Sorrow for sin and gratitude for the amazing mercy of God replace self-assertion, evasion of God and the soul's fallen motives. Optimum spiritual health simply involves remaining in the focused light of truth concerning our needs and their fulfillment in Jesus' redemptive work (1 John 1:5–7). An honest assessment of our spiritual state and a deepening trust in the Messiah are qualities which guarantee our continued spiritual growth.

"The heart which is illuminated by the Holy Spirit's application of truth is progressively set free from its bondage of sin and error ... As our hearts, the subconscious root of our personality, are increasingly filled with light, our minds are freed to discover and affirm truth, our wills are freed to obey God, and our emotions are released to feel about all things as God feels about them ... This fellowship will of course lead to works, to thoughts and words and acts on behalf of the kingdom of God. But these works will emerge primarily out of our fellowship with Christ. And we will be clearly aware that in the deepest sense they are his works and not ours—the acts of the risen Christ."[3]

The history of mankind is full of the fact that mankind in making gods in our own image have become less free. Your complaint might be one often voiced: If I AM is all loving, why would He allow or even command the death of so many people in the law and writings of the Tanakh (Old Testament)? The development of man's religion was a bloody, vicious, and enslaving circle of violence and human abuse. In ancient Canaan and surrounding societies, the worship of Baal and Molech included sacrificing of babies and young children; they were burned alive. The cannibalistic practice of eating one's children and the bloody sacrificing of young virgins were among the rituals of these religious communities. In addition, ancient temples were filled with enslaved prostitutes to use in the worship of gods that demanded impurity and enslavement. I AM, the three in one, stood against these withholding anger yet in loving-kindness and mercy holding out a different way a choice that the people were unwilling to make. They continually shunned His forgiveness. Genesis 6:5–6: "The LORD saw that the wickedness of man was great in the earth, and that every intention of the thoughts of his heart was only evil continually. And the LORD was sorry that he had made man on the earth, and it grieved him to his heart."

Yet I AM spares and forgives even if there are a few who still refrain from evil and continue to act rightly.

> Genesis 18:20–32: Then the LORD said, "Because the outcry against Sodom and Gomorrah is great and their sin is very grave, I will go down to see whether they have done altogether according to the outcry that has come to me. And if not, I will know." So the men turned from there and went toward Sodom, but Abraham still stood before the LORD. Then Abraham drew near and said, "Will you indeed sweep away the righteous with the wicked? Suppose there are fifty righteous within the city. Will you then sweep away the place and not spare it for the fifty righteous who are in it? Far be it from you to do such a thing, to put the righteous to death with the wicked, so that the righteous fare as the wicked! Far be that from you! Shall not the Judge of all the earth do what is just?" And the LORD said, "If I find at Sodom fifty righteous in the city, I will spare the whole place for their sake." Abraham answered and said, "Behold, I have

undertaken to speak to the Lord, I who am but dust and ashes. Suppose five of the fifty righteous are lacking. Will you destroy the whole city for lack of five?" And he said, "I will not destroy it if I find forty-five there." Again he spoke to him and said, "Suppose forty are found there." He answered, "For the sake of forty I will not do it." Then he said, "Oh let not the Lord be angry, and I will speak. Suppose thirty are found there." He answered, "I will not do it, if I find thirty there." He said, "Behold, I have undertaken to speak to the Lord. Suppose twenty are found there." He answered, "For the sake of twenty I will not destroy it." The leaders of Israel even fell into the entrapments of these horrific activities. Genesis Then he said, "Oh let not the Lord be angry, and I will speak again but this once. Suppose ten are found there." He answered, "For the sake of ten I will not destroy it."

Still mankind continues to go after destructive, deadly, vicious, and enslaving practices. 2 Kings 16:2–3: "Ahaz was twenty years old when he began to reign, and he reigned sixteen years in Jerusalem. And he did not do what was right in the eyes of the LORD his God, as his father David had done, but he walked in the way of the kings of Israel. He even burned his son as an offering, according to the despicable practices of the nations whom the LORD drove out before the people of Israel."

Jeremiah 7:30–36: "For the sons of Judah have done evil in my sight, declares the LORD. They have set their detestable things in the house that is called by my name, to defile it. And they have built the high places of Topheth, which is in the Valley of the Son of Hinnom, to burn their sons and their daughters in the fire," For the children of Israel and the children of Judah have done nothing but evil in my sight from their youth. The children of Israel have done nothing but provoke me to anger by the work of their hands, declares the LORD. This city has aroused my anger and wrath, from the day it was built to this day, so that I will remove it from my sight because of all the evil of the children of Israel and the children of Judah that they did to provoke me to anger—their kings and their officials, their priests and their prophets, the men of Judah and the inhabitants of Jerusalem. They have turned to me their back and not their face. And though I have taught them persistently, they have not listened to receive instruction. They set up their abominations in the house that is called by my name, to defile it. They built the high places of Baal in the Valley of the Son of Hinnom, to offer up their sons and daughters to Molech, though I did not command them, nor did it enter into my mind, that they should do this abomination, to cause Judah to sin. "Now therefore thus says the LORD, the God of Israel, concerning this city of which you say, 'It is given into the hand of the king of Babylon by sword, by famine, and by pestilence."

It would be completely against the character and nature of absolute love to not let the anger of His love destroy these evil cultures. Absolute love will not ignore or tolerate the injustice of the strong preying upon the weak. Absolute love defends the child, the widow, the fatherless, and the humble who cry out for His mighty arm to save them from evil men.

A. W. Tozer declares, "One mighty fact there is which for us men overwhelms all other considerations and gives significance to everything we do. It is that the human race has left its first estate and is morally fallen.

"Since the fall of man the earth has been a disaster area and everyone lives with a critical emergency. Nothing is normal. Everything is wrong and everyone is wrong until made right by the redeeming work of Christ and effective operation of the Holy Spirit.

"The universal disaster of the Fall compels us to think differently about our obligation to our fellow men. What would be entirely permissible under normal conditions becomes wrong in the present situation, and many things not otherwise required are necessary because of abnormal conditions.

"It is in view of this that all our Christian service must be evaluated. The needs of the people, not our own convenience, decide how far we should go and how much we shall do. Had there been no disaster there would have been no need for the Eternal Son to empty Himself and descend to Bethlehem's manger. Had there been no Fall there would have been no incarnation, no thorns, no cross. These resulted when divine goodness confronted the human emergency.

"While Christ was the perfect example of the healthy normal man, He yet did not live a normal life. He sacrificed many pure enjoyments to give Himself to the holy work of moral rescue. His conduct was determined not by what was legitimate or innocent, but by our human need. He pleased not Himself but lived for the emergency; and as He was so are we in this world.

"Before the judgment seat of Christ my service will be judged not by how much I have done but by how much I could have done. In God's sight my giving is measured not by how much I have given but by how much I could have given and how much I had left after my gift. The needs of the world and my total ability to minister to those needs decide the worth of my service.

"Not by its size is my gift judged, but by how much of me there is in it. No man gives at all until he has given all. No man gives anything acceptable to God until he has first given himself in love and sacrifice.

"The hero is sighted by his country not for the number of persons he has saved only, but for the degree of danger to himself present in his act. Service that can be done without peril, that carries no loss, no sacrifice, does not rate high in the sight of men or God.

"In the work of the church the amount one man must do to accomplish a given task is determined by how much or how little the rest of the company is willing to do. It is a rare church whose members all put their shoulders to the wheel. The typical church is composed of the few whose shoulders are bruised by their faithful labors and the many who are unwilling to raise a blister in the service of God and their fellow men. There may be a bit of wry humor in all this, but it is quite certain that there will be no laughter when each of us gives account to God of the deeds done in the body.

"I think that most Christians would be better pleased if the LORD did not inquire into their personal affairs too closely. They want Him to save them, keep them happy and take them to heaven at last, but not to be too inquisitive about their conduct or service. But He has searched us and known us; He knows our down sitting and our uprising and understands our thoughts afar off. There is no place to hide from those eyes that are as a flame of fire and there is no way to escape from the judgment of those feet that are fine brass. It is the part of wisdom to live with these things in mind."[4]

Instead of this enslavement, mankind was meant to be a steward and a servant. Man was to care for one another and the creation. In the beginning, I AM made a park or a garden for mankind. In it, man was to glorify I AM by enjoying Him forever. In the park was beauty untold and every plant and tree that was good for food. Genesis 2:15: "The LORD God took the man and put him in the garden of Eden to work it and keep it."

The Hebrew word for work in this voice also means "serve, worship, or cultivate" and the Hebrew word for keep also means "guard or protect." All things are from I AM and belong to I AM. We are free when we become what we were created for, to be worshipers of I AM and protectors of one another and the creation. We are free when we become more loving.

> John 8:31–36: So Jesus said to the Jews who had believed in him, "If you abide in my word, you are truly my disciples, and you will know the truth, and the truth will set you free." They answered him, "We are offspring of Abraham and have never been enslaved to anyone. How is it that you say, 'You will become free'?" Jesus answered them, "Truly, truly, I say to you, everyone who commits sin is a slave to sin. The slave does not remain

in the house forever; the son remains forever. So if the Son sets you free, you will be free indeed." Freedom is the characteristic outgrowth of believing that gives us the ability to set aside personal desires and postpone pleasure, (i.e. physical, emotional gratification), in order that we be liberated to find complete satisfaction in God and be separated from enslaving entanglements. Stewardship is the characteristic of believing that gives us the ability to be inter-connected with each other in a truly loving manner. We do not lose any integral parts of ourselves or disintegrate into another person, yet we value and need each other's gifts and uniqueness for the full use and completion of our own giftedness Servanthood is the characteristic of believing that gives us the ability to worship in everything that we do by looking to God to fill us and overflow through us into the lives of others for thoughtful attentiveness to God's desires for them.

R. C. Sproul writes, "How do we know if our faith is authentic? There are two basic tests for genuine faith. The first is our own inner disposition. A regenerate person has received the internal operation of the Holy Spirit, by which the inclination or disposition of the soul has been changed. The regenerate heart has a love and desire for Christ that is not found in the unbeliever ... In addition to the question of the heart, we must face the question of the presence or absence of the fruit of faith. Again, it is not a question of whether our fruit is perfect, but whether there is any fruit at all. No fruit means no faith. Some fruit means some faith. The Bible tells us we will know them by their fruit.

"The fruit we are looking for is the fruit of obedience ... This is where works fit into the Christian life. We are not justified by our works, but we are justified unto works. The indispensable evidence of true faith is the presence of works. The works add nothing to the merit of Christ, by whose merit we are justified. But faith inevitably and necessarily produces works or it is not saving faith ...

"Faith is shown or demonstrated by works. If no works are demonstrated, saving faith is absent. To have assurance of salvation we need objective evidence of the fruit in our lives. A regenerate person is a changed person. Two vital changes have taken place. The first change is a disposition of the soul affected by the Holy Spirit. The second change is the indwelling of the Spirit.

"If a person goes through two such alterations—regeneration and indwelling—it is simply impossible that there be no change in the individual's life. It is a root change, so radical that it is called a new creation. The change in the root produces change in the fruit."[5]

Romans 12:1: "I appeal to you therefore, brothers, by the mercies of God, to present your bodies as a living sacrifice, holy and acceptable to God, which is your spiritual worship." Absolute love transforms us to freely become captive to a life of sacrifice to others, serving others as a stewardship to I AM.

Kopshiy (freedom.) Exodus 21:2, 21:5, 21:26, 21:27, Deuteronomy 15:12, 15:13, 15:18, 1 Samuel 17:25, Job 3:19, 39:5, Psalm 88:5, **Isaiah 58:6,** Jeremiah 34:9, 34:10, 34:11, 34:14, 34:16 **Kapash** Leviticus 19:20.

Nakah (free, pure, clean, empty, exempt, innocent, acquitted.) Genesis 24:8, 24:41, Exodus 20:7, 21:19, 34:7, Numbers 5:19, 5:28, 5:31 ,14:18, Deuteronomy 5:11, Judges 15:3, 1 Samuel 26:9, 1 Kings 2:9, Job 9:28, 10:14, **Psalm 19:12, 19:13,** 51:2, Proverbs 6:29, 11:21, 16:5, 17:5, 19:5, 19:9, 28:20, Isaiah 3:26, Jeremiah 2:35, 25:29, 30:11, 46:28, 49:12, Joel 3:21, Nahum 1:3, Zechariah 5:3 **Nakiy** Genesis 24:41, 44:10, Exodus 21:28, 23:7, Numbers 32:22, Deuteronomy 19:10, 19:13, 21:8, 21:9, 24:5, 27:25, Joshua 2:17, 2:19, 2:20, 1 Samuel 19:5, 2 Samuel 3:28, 14:9, 1 Kings 15:22, 2 Kings 21:16, 24:4, Job 4:7, 9:23, 17:8, 22:19, 22:30, 27:17, Psalm 10:8, 15:5, **24:4,** 94:21, 106:38, Proverbs 1:11, 6:17, Isaiah 59:7, Jeremiah 2:34, **7:6,** 19:4, **22:3, 22:17,** 26:15, Joel 3:19, Jonah 1:14.

Eleutheria (freedom, liberty.) Romans 8:21, 1 Corinthians 7:39, 10:29, 2 Corinthians 3:17, Galatians 2:4, 5:1, 5:13, **James 1:25, 2:12, 1 Peter 2:16,**

2 Peter 2:19 Eleutheros (free, independent, not bound.) Matthew 17:26, **John 8:33, 8:36, Romans 6:20, 7:**3, 1 Corinthians 7:21, 7:22, 7:39, 9:1, 9:19, 12:13, **Galatians 3:28, 4:22, 4:23, 4:26, 4:30, 4:31**, Ephesians 6:8, Colossians 3:11, 1 Peter 2:16, Revelation 6:15, 13:16, 19:18 **Eleutheroo John 8:32, 8:36**, Romans 6:18, 6:22, **8:2, 8:21**, Galatians 5:1.

Abad (serve, work, obey, worship, cultivate, till.) **Genesis 2:5, 2:15, 3:23,** 4:2, 4:12, 14:4, 15:13, 15:14, 25:23, 27:29, 27:40, 29:15, 29:18, 29:20, 29:25, 29:27, 29:30, 30:26, 30:29, 31:6, 31:41, 49:15, Exodus 1:13, 1:14, 3:12, 4:23, 5:18, 6:5, 7:16, 8:1, 8:20, 9:1, 9:13, **10:3, 10:7, 10:8, 10:11, 10:24, 10:26,** 12:31, 13:5, 14:5, 14:12, **20:5, 20:9, 21:**2, 21:6, 23:24, 23:25, 23:33, Leviticus 25:39, 25:40, 25:46, Numbers 3:7, 3:8, **4:23, 4:24, 4:26, 4:30, 4:37, 4:41, 4:47, 7:**5, **8:11, 8:15, 8:19, 8:22, 8:25, 8:26,** 16:9, 18:6, 18:7, 18:21, 18:23, **Deuteronomy 4:19, 4:28, 5:9, 5:13, 6:13, 7:4, 7:16, 8:19, 10:12, 10:20, 11:13, 11:16, 12:2, 12:30, 13:2, 13:4, 13:6, 13:13, 15:12, 15:18.15:19, 17:3, 20:11, 21:3, 21:4, 28:14, 28:36, 28:39, 28:47, 28:48, 28:64, 29:18, 29:26, 30:17, 31:20,** Joshua 16:10, 22:5, 22:27, 23:7, 23:16, 24:2, 24:14, 24:15, 24:16, 24:18, 24:19, 24:20, 24:21, 24:22, 24:24, 24:31, Judges 2:7, 2:11, 2:13, 2:19, 3:6, 3:7, 3:8, 3:14, 9:28, 9:38, 10:6, 10:10, 10:13, 10:16, 1 Samuel 4:9, 7:3, 7:4, 8:8, 10:7, 11:1, 12:10, 12:14, 12:20, 12:24, 17:9, 26:19, 2 Samuel 9:10, 10:19, 15:8, 16:19, 22:44, 1 Kings 4:21, 9:6, 9:9, 9:21, 12:4, 12:7, 16:31, 22:53, 2 Kings 10:18, 10:19, 10:21, 10:22, 10:23, 17:12, 17:16, 17:33, 17:35, 17:41, 18:7, 21:3, 21:21, 25:24, 1 Chronicles 19:19, 28:9, 2 Chronicles 2:18, 7:19, 7:22, 10:4, 24:18, 30:8, 33:3, 33:16, 33:22, 34:33, 35:3, Nehemiah 9:35, Job 21:15, 36:11, 39:9, Psalm 2:11, 18:43 ,22:30, 72:11, 97:7, **100:2,** 102:22, 106:36, Proverbs 12:11, 28:19, Ecclesiastes 5:9, 5:12, Isaiah 14:3, 19:9, 19:21, 19:23, 28:21, 30:24, 43:23, 43:24, 60:12, Jeremiah 2:20, 5:19, 8:2, 11:10, 13:10, 16:11, 16:13, 17:4, 22:9, 22:13, 25:6, 25:11, 25:14, 27:6, 27:7, 27:8, 27:9, 27:11, 27:12, 27:13, 27:14, 27:17, 28:14, 30:8, 30:9, 34:9, 34:10, 34:14, 35:15, 40:9, 44:3, Ezekiel 20:39, 20:40, 29:18, 29:20, 34:27, 36:9, 36:34, 48:18, 48:19, Hosea 12:12, Zephaniah 3:9, Zechariah 2:9, 13:5, Malachi 3:14, 3:17, 3:18.

Douleuo (serve, obey.) Matthew 6:24, Luke 15:29, 16:13, John 8:33, Acts 7:7, 20:19, Romans 6:6, **7:6, 7:25,** 9:12, 12:11, 14:18, 16:18, Galatians 4:8.4:9,

4:25, 5:13, Ephesians 6:7, **Phil 2:22**, Colossians 3:24, 1 Thessalonians 1:9, 1 Timothy 6:2, Titus 3:3 **Doulos** Matthew 8:9.10:24, 10:25, 13:27, 13:28, 18:23, 18:26, 18:27, 18:28, 18:32, **20:27**, 21:34, 21:35, 21:36, 22:3, 22:4, 22:6, 22:8, 22:10, 24:45, 24:46 ,24:48, 24:5, 25:14, 25:19, 25:21, 25:23, 25:26, 25:30, 26:51, **Mark 10:44**, 12:2, 12:4, 13:34, 14:47, Luke 2:29, 7:2, 7:3, 7:8, 7:10, 12:37, 12:38, 12:43, 12:45, 12:46, 12:47, 14:17, 14:21, 14:22, 14:23, 15:22, 17:7, 17:9, 17:10, 19:13, 19:15, 19:17, 19:22, 20:10, 20:11, 22:50, John 4:51, 8:34, 8:35, 13:16, 15:15, 15:20, 18:10, 18:18, 18:26, Acts 2:18, 4:29, 16:17, Romans 1:1, 6:16, 6:17, 6:19, 6:20, 1 Corinthians 7:21, 7:22, 7:23, 12:13, 2 Corinthians 4:5, Galatians 1:10, 3:28, 4:1, 4:7, Ephesians 6:5, 6:6, 6:8, Phil 1:1, **2:7**, Colossians 3:11, 3:22, 4:1, 4:12, 1 Timothy 6:1, 2 Timothy 2:24, Titus 1:1, 2:9, Phile 1:16, James 1:1, 1 Peter 2:16, 2 Peter 1:1, 2:19, Jude 1:1, Revelation 1:1, 2:20, 6:15, 7:3, 10:7, 11:18, 13:16, 15:3, 19:2, 19:5, 19:18, 22:3, 22:6.

Latreuo (serve, worship.) Matthew 4:10, Luke 1:74, 2:37, 4:8, Acts 7:7, 7:42, 24:14, 26:7, 27:23, Romans 1:9, 1:25, Phil 3:3, 2 Timothy 1:3, **Hebrews 8:5, 9:9, 9:14,** 10:2, 12:28, 13:10, Revelation 7:15, 22:3.

Latreia John 16:2, Romans 9:4, **12:1, Hebrews 9:1, 9:6.**

Leitourgeo Acts 13:2, Romans 15:27, Hebrews 10:11 **Leitourgia** Luke 1:23, 2 Corinthians 9:12, **Phil 2:17, 2:30, Hebrews 8:6, 9:21 Leitourgos Romans 13:6,** 15:16, Phil 2:25, Hebrews 1:7, **8:2.**

Diakonia (serve, help, support, minister, care for, aid.) Luke 10:40, Acts 1:17, 1:25, **6:1, 6:4,** 11:29, 12:25, 20:24, 21:19, Romans 11:13, 12:7, 15:31, 1 Corinthians 12:5, 16:15, 2 Corinthians 3:7, 3:8, 3:9, 4:1, 5:18, 6:3, 8:4, 9:1, 9:12, 9:13, 11:8, Ephesians 4:12, Colossians 4:17, 1 Timothy 1:12, 2 Timothy 4:5, 4:11, Hebrews 1:14, Revelation 2:19 **Diakoneo** Matthew 4:11, 8:15, **20:28, 25:44,** 27:55, Mark 1:13, 1:31, 10:45, 15:41, Luke 4:39, 8:3, 10:40, 12:37, 17:8, 22:26, 22:27, John 12:2, 12:26, Acts 6:2, 19:22, Romans 15:25, 2 Corinthians 3:3, 8:19, 8:20, 1 Timothy 3:10, 3:13, 2 Timothy 1:18, Phile 1:13, Hebrews 6:10, 1 Peter 1:12, 4:10, 4:11.

End Notes

1. Fuller, Daniel P. *The Unity of the Bible: Unfolding God's Plan for Humanity.* 1992, pages 453–454.
2. Packer, J. I. *Truth and Power.* Harold Shaw Publishers, Wheaton, IL, 1996, pages 22–24.
3. Lovelace, Richard. *Renewal As a Way of Life: A Guide For Spiritual Growth.* Intervarsity Press, Downers Grove, IL, 1985, pages 134–135.
4. Tozer, A. W. *That Incredible Christian.* Christian Publications, Inc., Harrisburg, PA, 1964, 104–106.
5. Sproul, R. C. *The Soul's Quest for God: Satisfying the Hunger for Spiritual Communion with God.* 1992, pages 216–219.

CHAPTER TEN

Loyalty, Purity, and Justice

I AM, the three in one, is not a man-made idol. His anger cannot be appeased by anything we could do. There is nothing that we could give Him that He could need. There is no desire in Him for us to abuse others or be abused. Ezekiel 18:23: "Have I any pleasure in the death of the wicked, declares the Lord GOD, and not rather that he should turn from his way and live?"

Ezekiel 33:11: "Say to them, As I live, declares the Lord GOD, I have no pleasure in the death of the wicked, but that the wicked turn from his way and live; turn back, turn back from your evil ways, for why will you die, O house of Israel?" The sacrifices I AM, the three in one, instituted were to point to the gifts He gives, gifts of sustenance, forgiveness, cleansing, and life. The sacrifices prescribed were to point people to His care for them not as a means to gain His love. He is absolute love, love overflows from within. God's love is not based on outward perceived loveliness; loveliness is poured out on His beloved creation. We cannot win His love, we can only accept His love.

1 Samuel 15:22: "And Samuel said, 'Has the LORD as great delight in burnt offerings and sacrifices, as in obeying the voice of the LORD? Behold, to obey is better than sacrifice, and to listen than the fat of rams.'"

Psalm 40:6: "In sacrifice and offering you have not delighted, but you have given me an open ear. Burnt offering and sin offering you have not required." Psalm 50:23: "The one who offers thanksgiving as his sacrifice glorifies me; to one who orders his way rightly I will show the salvation of God!" Psalm 51:17: "The sacrifices of God are a broken spirit; a broken and contrite heart, O God, you will not despise." Proverbs 21:3: "To do righteousness and justice is more acceptable to the LORD than sacrifice."

The Tanakh (Old Testament) has five major offerings: burnt offering, meal offering, peace offering, sin offering, and the trespass offering. The offerings or sacrifices were to draw attention first to I AM and His forgiveness, second to His salvation from slavery, third to the provisions He supplies, fourth to the peace and rest that He brings, and fifth to the relationships that He restores. However two specific things about the details of how these acts of worship were to be performed pointed to a further mystery not yet revealed. The perfection or unblemished nature of the animals sacrificed or the grains offered pointed to the need of a perfect, unblemished sacrifice that had to be made. Secondly, it was to be of the firstborn of the animals or the firstfruits of the harvest that were required, which pointed to the need for a totally unique nature that belonged to the offering. As the only one of its kind, the firstborn, there can only be one firstborn.

The offerings were to be orderly and worshipful, sanctifying and cleansing, but not abusive or cruel. If a bull was not available or could not be afforded, a lamb could be offered; if not a lamb then a goat; and if not a goat then a bird. The point of the offering was for the person to see the provision of I AM not to gain favor. The favor was found in the worshipful and grateful attitude of the offering. I AM desired to give them all that was needed. Psalm 37:4: "Delight yourself in the LORD, and he will give you the desires of your heart." Psalm 147:10–11: "His delight is not in the strength of the horse, nor his pleasure in the legs of a man, but the LORD takes pleasure in those who fear him, in those who hope in his steadfast love."

Louis Berkhof writes, "On the one hand the covenant is unconditional. There is in the covenant of grace no condition that can be considered meritorious ...

"On the other hand the covenant may be called conditional. There is a sense in which the covenant is conditional. If we consider the basis of the covenant, it is clearly conditional on the surety of Jesus Christ. In order to introduce the covenant of grace, Christ had to, and actually did, meet the conditions originally laid down in the covenant of works, by his active and passive obedience. Again, it may be said that the covenant is conditional as far as the first conscious entrance into the covenant as a real communion of life is concerned. This entrance is contingent on faith, a faith, however, which is itself a gift of God."[1]

The contrast between the love and care of I AM and the bloodthirsty, abusive, enslaving cultures in the ancient Near East is stark. It is amazing that I AM must constantly warn not to follow after those brutal uncaring ways of making idols that we can serve rather than follow after Him. 2 Kings 17:15: "They despised his statutes and his covenant that he made with their fathers and the warnings that he gave them. They went after false idols and became false, and they followed the nations that were around them, concerning whom the LORD had commanded them that they should not do like them."

Abuse tears at the very nature of the one being abused as well as the abuser. There is a logical disconnect between reality and what is experienced while abusing someone or being abused by someone. It is common for psychiatrists and psychologists to talk about dissociative disorders. Dissociative orders or syndromes are characterized by disruptions or lapses, long or short, in consciousness, identity, memory, motor behavior, and environmental awareness. People literally become torn apart or not themselves from abusing and being abused. Sometimes the abuse is buried latent deep inside so that it is not even remembered by the one who was abused, only to know that something is terribly wrong but not consciously being able to face or deal with whatever it might be. Sometimes multiple selves emerge. Often abused individuals end up abusing others. Of course that is all in the past? No one knows of idol worshippers who sacrifice or eat their own children? No one knows of people forced into slavery and prostitution as temple worship?

Today it is estimated by UNICEF that there are 1.2 million people kidnapped and sold into human trafficking every year. The majority of those taken are between the ages of eighteen and twenty-four years old, and 95 percent are taken for the purpose of physically abusive labor or sexual violence. Every nine seconds in the United States alone a woman is assaulted or beaten. There are ninety-five thousand rapes reported each year in the United States and no one knows how many go unreported. Minnesota Citizens Concerned For Life reports that in the United States a baby is aborted every twenty-six seconds. Five children die each day of child abuse and child neglect.[2]

Sexual gratification is not an end in itself and at the same time it is not a means to initiate or establish a relationship. Love is not sex and sexual gratification is not love.

Sexual intercourse is a gift from I AM and He established its bounds— the bounds of one committed, caring relationship of a man to a woman. In the garden there was one man and one woman made one flesh, and it was very good. This was the pattern of goodness and love, yet sexual union is one of the gifts of I AM that is most perverted by people in our world.

It is clear in nature that sexual gratification, though achievable, was not designed by the creator to be male with male, or female with female, or in an unloving, uncommitted relationship male to female. Learning that whatever feels good is not necessarily good is a part of becoming a loving and caring individual.

Sexual sin is a unique form of sin because it is within our bodies. 1 Corinthians 6:18–20: "Flee from sexual immorality. Every other sin a person commits is outside the body, but the sexually immoral person sins against his own body. Or do you not know that your body is a temple of the Holy Spirit within you, whom you have from God? You are not your own, for you were bought with a price. So glorify God in your body."

Sexual union only is safe and sanctioned by this one flesh relationship, in lifelong commitment of one man to one woman. This relationship was uniquely to image forth I AM and His relationship to us. Ephesians 5:31–32: "Therefore a man shall leave his father and mother and hold fast to his wife, and the two shall become one flesh. This mystery is profound, and I am saying that it refers to Christ and the church."

It is difficult to find anyone these days who is not touched by the devastating effects of divorce, the tearing apart of families, and damage to children of broken relationships. What is holding the fabric of purity and justice together in this world? Pope John Paul II wrote, "Today, as a result of advances in medicine and in a cultural context frequently closed to the transcendent, the experience of dying is marked by new features. When the prevailing tendency is to value life only to the extent that it brings pleasure and well-being, suffering seems like an unbearable setback, something from which one must be freed at all costs. Death is considered 'senseless' if it suddenly interrupts a life still open to a future of new and interesting experiences. But it becomes a "rightful liberation" once life is held to be no longer meaningful because it is filled with pain and inexorably doomed to even greater suffering.

"Furthermore, when he denies or neglects his fundamental relationship to God, man thinks he is his own rule and measure, with the right to demand that society should guarantee him the ways and means of deciding what to do with his life in full and complete autonomy. It is especially people in the developed countries who act in this way: they feel encouraged to do so also by the constant progress of medicine and its ever more advanced techniques. By using highly sophisticated systems and equipment, science and medical practice today are able not only to attend to cases formerly considered untreatable and to reduce or eliminate pain, but also to sustain and prolong life even in situations of extreme frailty, to resuscitate artificially patients whose basic biological functions have undergone collapse and to use special procedures to make organs available for transplanting.

"In this context the temptation grows to have recourse to euthanasia, that is, to take control of death and bring it about before its time, 'gently' ending one's own life or the life of others. In reality, what might seem logical and humane, when looked at more closely is seen to be senseless and inhumane. Here we are faced with one of the more alarming symptoms of the 'culture of death,' which is advancing above all in prosperous societies, marked by an attitude of excessive preoccupation with efficiency and which sees the growing number of elderly and disabled people as intolerable and too burdensome. These people are very isolated by their families and by society, which are organized almost exclusively on the basis of criteria of productive efficiency, according to which a hopelessly impaired life no longer has value ...

"Quite different from this is the way of love and true mercy, which our common humanity calls for, and upon which faith in Christ the Redeemer, who died and rose again, sheds ever new light. The request which arises from the human heart in the supreme confrontation with suffering and death, especially when faced with the temptation to give up in utter desperation, is above all a request for companionship, sympathy and support in time of trial. It is a plea for help to keep on hoping when all human hopes fail ...

"This natural aversion to death and this incipient hope of immortality are illumined and brought to fulfillment by Christian faith, which both promises and offers a share in the victory of the Risen Christ: it is the victory of the One who, by his redemptive death, has set man free from death, 'the wages of sin' (Rom. 6:23), and has given him the Spirit, the pledge of the resurrection and of life (cf. Rom. 8:11). The certainty of future immortality and hope in the promised resurrection cast new light on the mystery of suffering and death, and fill the believer with an extraordinary capacity to trust fully in the plan of God."[3]

I AM, the three in one, keeps loyalty and faithfulness. He is slow to anger and forgives rebellion, perversion, and unfaithfulness, but He will not let the guilty go unpunished. He is overflowing with loving-kindness and mercy. Yet He will have mercy upon who He will have mercy. Deuteronomy 10:17–20: "For the LORD your God is God of gods and Lord of lords, the great, the mighty, and the awesome God, who is not partial and takes no bribe. He executes justice for the fatherless and the widow, and loves the sojourner, giving him food and clothing. love the sojourner, therefore, for you were sojourners in the land of Egypt. You shall fear the LORD your God. You shall serve him and hold fast to him, and by his name you shall swear."

Psalm 10:17–18: "O LORD, you hear the desire of the afflicted; you will strengthen their heart; you will incline your ear to do justice to the fatherless and the oppressed, so that man who is of the earth may strike terror no more."

James 1:27: "Religion that is pure and undefiled before God, the Father, is this: to visit orphans and widows in their affliction, and to keep oneself unstained from the world." The absolute love of I AM is just that absolute. It cannot be earned, but it is demanding and just. It is not unconditional it is uncompromising, sacrificial and absolute. We cannot do a thing to deserve His forgiveness, but justice demands repayment.

The offerings I AM required in the Tanakh though point to His forgiveness, His salvation from slavery, the provisions He supplies, the peace and rest that He brings, and the relationships that He restores. He provides the sacrifice, the perfect and only sacrifice He could accept.

> Hebrews 9:11–28: But when Christ appeared as a high priest of the good things that have come, then through the greater and more perfect tent (not made with hands, that is, not of this creation) he entered once for all into the holy places, not by means of the blood of goats and calves but by means of his own blood, thus securing an eternal redemption. For if the blood of goats and bulls, and the sprinkling of defiled persons with the ashes of a heifer, sanctify for the purification of the flesh, how much more will the blood of Christ, who through the eternal Spirit offered himself without blemish to God, purify our conscience from dead works to serve the living God. Therefore he is the mediator of a new covenant, so that those who are called may receive the promised eternal inheritance, since a death has occurred that redeems them from the transgressions committed under the first covenant. For where a will is involved, the death of the

one who made it must be established. For a will takes effect only at death, since it is not in force as long as the one who made it is alive. Therefore not even the first covenant was inaugurated without blood. For when every commandment of the law had been declared by Moses to all the people, he took the blood of calves and goats, with water and scarlet wool and hyssop, and sprinkled both the book itself and all the people, saying, "This is the blood of the covenant that God commanded for you." And in the same way he sprinkled with the blood both the tent and all the vessels used in worship. Indeed, under the law almost everything is purified with blood, and without the shedding of blood there is no forgiveness of sins. Thus it was necessary for the copies of the heavenly things to be purified with these rites, but the heavenly things themselves with better sacrifices than these. For Christ has entered, not into holy places made with hands, which are copies of the true things, but into heaven itself, now to appear in the presence of God on our behalf. Nor was it to offer himself repeatedly, as the high priest enters the holy places every year with blood not his own, for then he would have had to suffer repeatedly since the foundation of the world. But as it is, he has appeared once for all at the end of the ages to put away sin by the sacrifice of himself. And just as it is appointed for man to die once, and after that comes judgment, so Christ, having been offered once to bear the sins of many, will appear a second time, not to deal with sin but to save those who are eagerly waiting for him.

Moses and the Tanakh point to Jesus Christ, Isa AL-Masih, Yeshua the long awaited Messiah. He is one who makes all things new, who has satisfied the justice of I AM by taking on the robes of humanity and humility. This is what absolute love is. I AM, the three in one, is actively loyal to His creation and His beloved creatures, He restores purity because He is pure and brings about justice because He is absolutely just.

> 2 Corinthians 5:14-21: For the love of Christ controls us, because we have concluded this: that one has died for all, therefore all have died; and he died for all, that those who live might no longer live for themselves but for him who for their sake died and was raised. From now on, therefore, we regard no one according to the flesh. Even though we once regarded Christ according to the flesh, we regard him thus no longer. Therefore, if anyone is in Christ, he is a new creation. The old has passed away; behold, the new has come. All this is from God, who through Christ reconciled us to himself and gave us the ministry of reconciliation; that is, in Christ God was reconciling the world to himself, not counting their trespasses against them, and entrusting to us the message of reconciliation. Therefore, we are ambassadors for Christ, God making his appeal through us. We implore you on behalf of Christ, be reconciled to God. For our sake he made him to be sin who knew no sin, so that in him we might become the righteousness of God.

Jesus, Isa Al-Misah, Yeshua the promised Messiah, is now our perfect mediator and way to purity, wholeness, and integrity, our way to being made whole.

> Hebrews 7:22-28: This makes Jesus the guarantor of a better covenant. The former priests were many in number,—were prevented by death from continuing in office, but he holds his priesthood permanently, because he continues forever. Consequently, he is able to save to the uttermost those who draw near to God through him, since he always lives to make intercession for them. For it

was indeed fitting that we should have such a high priest, holy, innocent, unstained, separated from sinners, and exalted above the heavens. He has no need, like those high priests, to offer sacrifices daily, first for his own sins and then for those of the people, since he did this once for all when he offered up himself." For the law appoints men in their weakness as high priests, but the word of the oath, which came later than the law, appoints a Son who has been made perfect forever.

Without the absolute love of I AM, the three in one, justice would fade and die and purity and wholeness would disappear. John 1:14: "And the Word became flesh and dwelt among us, and we have seen his glory, glory as of the only Son from the Father, full of grace and truth."

Loyalty is the characteristic outgrowth of believing that gives us the ability to remain true or faithful to I AM, ourselves, and others so that we are not pushed or led along by demands other than God's.

Purity is the characteristic outgrowth of believing that gives us the ability to be unmixed in our allegiance toward God so that we won't be driven by any other purpose than to love, glorify, and enjoy God to the ultimate benefit, enjoyment, and fulfillment of ourselves and others.

Justice is the characteristic outgrowth of believing that gives us the ability to act rightly on behalf of God so that despots (those who want to control, oppress, and use others for personal gain) are not allowed to triumph and the defenseless are defended.

Bernard of Clairvaux has written, "Nothing can be so restless and fleeting—no part of my nature can be so changeful—than my heart. How exceedingly vain, trifling and unsettled is this vagabond. Never fixed on the will of God, never stirred by divine guidance and counsel, it follows instead its own whims. It is in perpetual motion, without any principle of rest within it. It is under a thousand different determinations at once and flies about after innumerable quests. It makes experiments but to no purpose. It seeks rest everywhere lies away from but it finds it not. Happiness flies away from it ...

"So when the soul falls away from worthy causes, and it becomes bewildered by sordid affections- then vanity seizes it, curiosity distracts it, covetous desires allure it, pleasure seduces it, luxury defiles it, envy racks it, anger ruffles it and grief afflicts and depresses it. The soul is then overwhelmed and sinks into all manner of vice. All this happens because it forsakes God, for He alone is the answer to all the heart's wants and desires. Thus the mind is dissipated and scattered among a multitude of trifles. Although it seeks anxiously for satisfaction, yet it cannot attain any until it returns to the All-Sufficient object of the heart ...

"The conditions of my being are such that I cannot live in subjection to myself but only in being subject to Him. I can never have the mastery of my own heart. Only God has that. So long, then, as I am not united to God, I am divided within myself and at perpetual strife within myself. Now this union with God can only love. And the subjection to Him can only be grounded in humility. And the humility can only be the result of knowing and believing the truth, that is to say, having the right notions of God and of myself.

"How necessary it is to inquire diligently about the true state of my soul. Then I will discover how vile, weak, fickle, and corruptible I am. Then I will discover also how vital t is to lay hold of God and to hold Him fast, for it is from Him that I derive my being and without Whom I am nothing."[4]

Emet (loyal, true, trustworthy, firm, faithful, reliable, stable, certain.) Genesis 24:27, 24:48, 24:49, 32:10, 42:16, 47:29, Exodus 18:21, 34:6, Deuteronomy 13:14, 17:4, 22:20, Joshua 2:12, 2:14, 24:14, Judges 9:15, 9:16, 9:19, 1 Samuel 12:24, 2 Samuel 2:6, 7:28, 15:20, 1 Kings 2:4, 3:6, 10:6, 17:24, 22:16, 2 Kings 20:3, 20:19, 2 Chronicles 9:5, 15:3, 18:15, 31:20, 32:1, Nehemiah 7:2, 9:13, 9:33, Esther 9:30, Psalm **15:2**, 19:9, 25:5, 25:10, 26:3, 30:9, 31:5, 40:10, 40:11, 43:3, 45:4, **51:6**, 54:5, 57:3, 57:10, 61:7, 69:13, 71:22, 85:10, 85:11, 86:11, 86:15, 89:14, 91:4, 108:4, 111:7, 111:8, 115:1, 117:2, 119:43, 119:142, 119:151, 119:160, 132:11, 138:2, 145:18, 146:6, Proverbs 3:3, 8:7, 11:18, 12:19, 14:22, 14:25, **16:6**, 20:28, 22:21, 23:23, 29:14, Ecclesiastes 12:10, Isaiah 10:20, 16:5, 38:3, 38:18, 38:19, 39:8, 42:3,

43:9, 48:1, 59:14, 59:15, 61:8, Jeremiah 2:21, 4:2, 9:5, 10:10, 14:13, 23:28, 26:15, 28:9, 32:41, 33:6, 42:5, **Ezekiel 18:8, 18:9**, Daniel 8:12, 8:26, 9:13, 10:1, 10:21, 11:2, Hosea 4:1, Micah 7:20, Zechariah 7:9, 8:3, 8:8, 8:16, 8:19, Malachi 2:6.

Aletheia (loyal, true, dependable, upright, fidelity, real.) Matthew 22:16, 5:33, 12:14, 12:32, Luke 4:25, 20:21, 22:59, John 1:14, 1:17, 3:21, **4:23, 4:24**, 5:33, **8:32, 8:40, 8:44, 8:45, 8:46**, 14:6, 14:17, 15:26, 16:7, 16:13, 17:17, 17:19, 18:37, 18:38, Acts 4:27, 10:34, 26:25, Romans 1:18, 1:25, 2:2, 2:8, 2:20, 3:7, 9:1, 15:8, 1 Corinthians 5:8, **13:6**, 2 Corinthians 4:2, 6:7, 7:14, 11:10, 12:6, 13:8, Galatians 2:5, 2:14, 3:1, 5:7, Ephesians 1:13, 4:21, 4:24, 2 Thessalonians 2:10, 2:12, 2:13, 1 Timothy 2:4, 2:7, 3:15, 4:3, 6:5, 2 Timothy 2:15, 2:18, 2:25, **3:7, 3:8, 4:4**, Titus 1:1, 1:14, Hebrews 10:26, James 1:18, 3:14, 5:19, 1 Peter 1:22, 2 Peter 1:12, 2:2, **1 John 1:6, 1:8, 2:4, 2:21, 3:18, 3:19, 4:6, 5:6**, 2 John 1:1, 1:2, 1:3, 1:4, 3 John 1:1, 1:3, 1:4, 1:8, 1:12

Alethes (honest, genuine.) Matthew 22:16, Mark 12:14, 3:33, 4:18, 5:31, 5:32, 7:18, 8:13, 8:14, 8:16, 8:17, 8:26, 10:41, 19:35, 21:24, Acts 12:9, Romans 3:4, 2 Corinthians 6:8, Phil 4:8, Titus 1:13, 1 Peter 5:12, 2 Peter 2:22, **1 John 2:8, 2:27**, 3 John 1:12 **Alethinos** Luke 16:11, John 1:9, 4:23, 4:37, 6:32, 7:28, 15:1, 17:3, 19:35, 1 Thessalonians 1:9, Hebrews 8:2, 9:24, 10:22, **1 John 2:8, 5:20**, Revelation 3:7, 3:14, 6:10, 15:3, 16:7, 19:2, 19:9, 19:11, 21:5, 22:6.

Taher (purity, empty, bright, clean.) Genesis 35:2 Leviticus 11:32, 12:7, 12:8, 13:6, 13:13, 13:17, 13:23, 13:28, 13:34, 13:37, 13:58, 13:59, 14:4, 14:7, 14:8, 14:9, 14:11, 14:14, 14:17, 14:18, 14:19, 14:20, 14:25, 14:28, 14:29, 14:31, 14:48, 14:53, 15:13, 15:28, 16:19, 16:30, 17:15, 22:4, 22:7, 23:22, Numbers 8:6, 8:7, 8:15, 8:21, 19:12, 19:19, 31:23, 31:24, Joshua 22:17, 2 Kings 5:10, 5:12, 5:13, 5:14, 2 Chronicles 29:15, 29:16, 29:18, 30:18, 34:3, 34:5, 34:8, Ezra 6:20, Nehemiah 12:30, 13:9, 13:22, 13:30, Job 4:17, 17:9, 37:21, **Psalm 51:7**, Proverbs 20:9, Isaiah 66:17, Jeremiah 13:27, 33:8, Ezekiel 22:24, 24:13, 36:25, 36:33, 37:23, 39:12, 39:14, 39:16, 43:26, Malachi 3:3, **Tehowr** Proverbs 22:11.

Hagnos (purity, holiness, innocence, chaste.) 2 Corinthians 7:11, 11:2, **Phil 1:16, 4:8**, 1 Timothy 5:22, Titus 2:5, James 3:17, 1 Peter 3:2, **1 John 3:3**

Hagnotes (purity, sincerity.) 2 Corinthians 6:6 **Hagneia** 1 Timothy 4:12, 5:2.

Katharos (purity, clean, clear, free, guiltless.) **Matthew 5:8, 8:**2, 8:3, 23:26, 27:59, Luke 11:41, John 13:10, 13:11, 15:3, Acts 18:6, 20:26, Romans 14:20, **1 Timothy 1:5**, 3:9, 2 Timothy 1:3, 2:22, Titus 1:15, **Hebrews 10:22**, **James 1:27** ,**1 Peter 1:22**, Revelation 15:6, 19:8, 19:14, 21:18, 21:21, 22:1, **Katharizo** (purify, cleanse, remove) Matthew 8:2, 8:3, 10:8, 11:5, 23:25, 23:26, Mark 1:40, 1:41, 1:42, 7:19, Luke 4:27, 5:12, 5:13, 7:22, 11:39, 17:14, 17:17, Acts 10:15, 11:9, 15:9, 2 Corinthians 7:1, **Ephesians 5:26**, **Titus 2:14**, **Hebrews 9:14, 9:22, 9:23**, **James 4:8**, 1 John 1:**7, 1:9 Katharotes,** Hebrews 9:13, **Katharismos** Mark 1:44, Luke 2:22, 5:14, John 2:6, 3:25, **Hebrews 1:3**, 2 Peter 1:9.

Zedakah (righteousness, executed justice, truthfulness, justification, salvation, prosperous.) Genesis 15:6, 18:19, 30:33, Deuteronomy 6:25, 9**:4, 9:5, 9:6**, 24:13, 33:21, Judges 5:11, 1 Samuel 12:7, 26:23, 2 Samuel 8:15, 19:28, 22:21, 22:25, 1 Kings 3:6, 8:32, 10:9, 1 Chronicles 18:14, 2 Chronicles 6:23, 9:8, Nehemiah 2:20, 27:6, 33:26, Job 35:8, 37:23, Psalm 5:8, 11:7, 22:31, 24:5, 31:1, 33:5, 36:6, 36:10, 40:10, 51:14, 69:27, 71:2, 71:15, 71:16, 71:19, 71:24, 72:1, 72:3, 88:12, 89:16, 98:2, 99:4, 103:6, 103:17, 106:3, 106:31, 111:3, 112:3, 112:9, 119:40, 119:142, 143:1, 143:11, 145:7, Proverbs 8:18, 8:20, 10:2, 11:4, 11:5, 11:6, 11:18, 11:19, 12:28, 13:6, 14:34, 15:9, 16:8, 16:12, 16:31, 21:3, 21:21, Isaiah 1:27, 5:7, 5:16, 5:23, 9:7, 10:22, 28:17, 32:16, 32:17, **33:5, 33:15,** 45:8, 45:23, 45:24, 46:12, 46:13, 48:1, 48:18, 51:6, 51:8, **54:14, 54:17,** 56:1, 57:12, 58:2, 59:9, 59:14, 59:16, 59:17, 60:17, 61:10, 61:11, 63:1, 64:6, Jeremiah 4:2, 9:24, 22:3, 22:15, 23:5, 33:15, 51:10, Ezekiel 3:20, 14:14, 14:20, 18:5, 18:19, 18:20, 18:21, 18:22, 18:24, 18:26, 18:27, 33:12, 33:13, 33:14, 33:16, 33:18, 33:19, 45:9, Daniel 9:7, 9:16, 9:18, Hosea 10:12, Joel 2:23, Amos 5:7, 5:24, 6:12, Micah 6:5, 7:9, Zechariah 8:8, Malachi 3:3, 4:2.

Mispat (justice, litigate, decision, sentence, right, rectify, proper, fit.)
Genesis 18:19, 18:25, 40:13, Exodus 15:25, 21:1, 21:9, 21:31, 23:6, 24:3,
26:30, 28:15, 28:29, 28:30, Leviticus 5:10, 9:16, 18:4, 18:5, 18:26, 19:15,
19:35, 19:37, 20:22, 24:22, 25:18, 26:15.26:43, 26:46, Numbers 9:3, 9:14,
15:16, 15:24, 27:5, 27:11, 27:21, 29:6, 29:18 ,29:21, 29:24, 29:27, 29:30,
29:33, 29:37, 35:12, 35:24, 35:29, 36:13, Deuteronomy 1:17, 4:1, 4:5, 4:8,
4:14, 4:45, 5:1, 5:31, 6:1, 6:20, 7:11, 7:12, 8:11, **10:18,** 11:1, 11:32, 12:1,
16:18, 16:19, 17:8, 17:9, 17:11, 18:3, 21:17, 24:17, 25:1, 26:16, 26:17, 27:19,
30:16, 32:4, 32:41, 33:10, 33:21, Joshua 6:15, 20:6, 24:25, Judges 4:5, 13:12,
18:7, 1 Samuel 2:13, 8:3, 8:9, 8:11, 10:25.30:25, 2 Samuel 8:15, 15:2, 15:4,
15:6, 22:23, 1 Kings 2:3, 3:11, 3:28, 4:28, 6:12, 6:38, 7:7, 8:45, 8:49, 8:58,
8:59, 9:4, 10:9, 11:33, 18:28, 20:40, 2 Kings 1:7, 11:14, 17:26, 17:27, 17:33,
17:34 ,17:37, 17:40, 25:6, 1 Chronicles 6:32, 15:13, 16:1, 16:14, 18:14,
22:13, 23:31, 24:19, 28:7, 2 Chronicles 4:7, 4:20, 6:35, 6:39, 7:17, 8:14, 9:8,
19:6, 19:8, 19:10, 30:16, 33:8, 35:13, Ezra 3:4, 7:10, Nehemiah 1:7, 8:18,
9:13, 9:29, 10:29, Job 8:3, 9:19, 9:32, 13:18, 14:3, 19:7, 22:4, 23:4, 27:2,
29:14, 31:13, 32:9, 34:4, 34:5, 34:6, 34:12, 34:17, 34:23, 35:2, 36:6, 36:17,
37:23, 40:8, Psalm 1:5, 7:6, 9:4, 9:7, 9:16, 10:5, 17:2, 18:22, 19:9, **25:9, 33:5,**
35:23, 36:6, 37:6, 37:28, 37:30, 48:11, 72:1, 72:2, 76:9, 81:4, **89:14, 89:30,**
94:15, 97:2, 97:8, 99:4, 101:1, 103:,105:5, 105:7, 106:3, 111:7, 112:5, 119:7,
119:13, 119:20, 119:30, 119:39, 119:43, 119:52, 119:62, 119:75, 119:84,
119:91, 119:102, 119:106, 119:108, 119:120, 119:121, 119:132, 119:137,
119:149, 119:156, 119:160, 119:164, 119:175, 122:5, 140:12, 143:2, **146:7,**
147:19, 147:20, 149:9, Proverbs 1:3, 2:8, 2:9, 8:20, 12:5, 13:23, 16:8, 16:10,
16:11, 16:33, 17:23, 18:,19:28, 21:3, 21:7 ,21:15, 24:23, 28:5, 29:4, 29:26,
Ecclesiastes 3:16, 5:8, 8:5, 8:6, 11:9, 12:14, **Isaiah 1:17, 1:21, 1:27,** 3:14,
4:4, 5:7, 5:16, 9:7, 10:2, 16:5, **26:8, 26:9,** 28:6, 28:17, 28:26, 30:18, 32:1,
32:7, 32:16, 33:5, 34:5, 40:14, 40:27, 41:1, 42:1, 42:3, 42:4, 49:4, 50:8,
51:4, 53:8, 54:17, 56:1, 58:2, 59:8, 59:9, 59:11, 59:14, 59:15, 61:8, Jeremiah
1:16, 4:2, 4:12, 5:1, 5:4, 5:5, 5:28, 7:5, 8:7, 9:24, 10:24, 12:1, 17:11, 21:12,
22:3, 22:13, 22:15, 23:5, 30:11, 30:18, 32:7, 32:8, 33:15, 39:5, 46:28, 48:21,
48:47, 49:12, 51:9, 52:9, Lamentations 3:35, 3:59, Ezekiel 5:6, 5:7, 5:8, 7:23,
7:27, 11:12, 11:20, 16:38, 18:5, 18:8, 18:9, 18:17, 18:19, 18:21, 18:27, 20:11,
20:13, 20:16, 20:18, 20:19, 20:2, 20:24, 20:25, 21:27, 22:29, 23:24, 23:45,

33:14, 33:16, 33:19, 34:16, 36:27, 37:24, 39:21, 42:11, 44:24, 45:9, Daniel 9:5, Hosea 2:19, 5:1, 5:11, 6:5, 10:4, 12:6, Amos 5:7, 5:15, 5:24, 6:12, Micah 3:1, 3:8, 3:9, 6:8, 7:9, Habakkuk 1:4, 1:7, 1:12, Zephaniah 2:,3:5, 3:8, 3:15, Zechariah 7:9, 8:16, Malachi 2:17, 3:5, 4:4.

Krino (justice, separate, distinguish, select, prefer, think, consider, decide, propose, Intend, Condemn, Criticize) Matthew 5:40, 7:1, 7:2, 19:28, Luke 6:37, 7:43, 12:57, 19:22, 22:30, John **3:17, 3:18, 5:**22, 5:30, 7:24, 7:51, 8:15, 8:16, 8:26, 8:50, 12:47, 12:48, 16:11, 18:31, Acts 3:13, 4:19, 7:7, 13:27, 13:46, 15:19, 16:4, 16:15, 17:31, 20:16, 21:25, 23:3, 23:6 ,24:6, 24:21, 25:9, 25:10, 25:20, 25:25, 26:6, 26:8, 27:1, **Romans 2:1, 2:3, 2:12, 2:16, 2:27,** 3:4, 3:6, 3:7, **14:3, 14:4, 14:5, 14:10, 14:13, 1** Corinthians 2:2, 4:5, 5:3, 5:12, 5:13, 6:1, 6:2, 6:3, 6:6, 7:37, 10:15, 10:29, 11:13, 11:31, 11:32, 2 Corinthians 2:1, 5:14, Colossians 2:16, 2 Thessalonians 2:12, 2 Timothy 4:1, 3:12, Hebrews 10:30, 13:4, **James 2:12, 4:11, 4:12, 1** Peter 1:17, 2:23, 4:5, 4:6, Revelation 6:10, 11:18, 16:5, 18:8, 18:20, 19:2, 19:11, 20:12, 20:13 **Krisis** Matthew 5:21, 5:22, 10:15, 11:22, 11:24, 12:18, 12:20, 12:36, 12:41, 12:42, 23:23, 23:33, Mark 3:29, 6:11, Luke 10:14, 11:31, 11:32, 11:42, John 3:19, 5:22, 5:24, 5:27, 5:29, 5:30, 7:24, 8:16, 12:31, 16:8, 16:11, Acts 8:33, 2 Thessalonians 1:5, 1 Timothy 5:24, Hebrews 9:27, 10:27, **James 2:13, 2** Peter 2:4, 2:9, 2:11, 3:7, 1 **John 4:17,** Jude 1:6, 1:9, 1:15, Revelation 14:7, 16:7, 18:10, 19:2.

Dikaiosune (righteousness, uprightness, justice.) Matthew 3:15, 5:6, 5:10, 5:20, 6:33, 21:32, Luke 1:75, John 16:8, 16:10, Acts 10:35, 13:10, 17:31, 24:25, Romans 1:17, **3:5, 3:21, 3:22, 3:25, 3:26, 4:3, 4:5, 4:6, 4:9, 4:11, 4:13, 4:22, 5:17, 5:21, 6:13, 6:16, 6:18, 6:19, 6:20,** 8:10, 9:28, 9:30, 9:31, 10:3, 10:4, 10:5, 10:6, 10:1, 14:17, 1 Corinthians 1:30, 2 Corinthians 3:9, 5:21, 6:7, 6:14, 9:9, 9:10, 11:15, **Galatians 2:21, 3:6, 3:21, 5:**5, Ephesians 4:24, 5:9, 6:14, Phil 1:11, 3:6, 3:9, 1 Timothy 6:11, 2 Timothy 2:22, 3:16, 4:8, Titus 3:5, Hebrews 1:9, 5:13, 7:2, 11:7, 11:33, 12:11, James 1:20, 2:23, 3:18, 1 Peter 2:24, 3:14, 2 Peter 1:1, 2:5, 2:21, 3:13, 1 **John 2:29, 3:7, 3:10,** Revelation 19:11

Dikaioo (acquitted, made free, made pure, proved to be right.) Matthew 11:19, 12:37, Luke 7:29, 7:35, 10:29, 16:15, 18:14, Acts 13:39, Romans 2:13, **3:4, 3:20, 3:24, 3:26, 3:28, 3:30, 4:2, 4:5, 5:1, 5:9, 6:7,** 8:30, 8:33, 1 Corinthians 4:4, 6:11, Galatians 2:16, 2:17, 3:8, 3:11, 3:24, 5:4, 1 Timothy 3:16, Titus 3:7, James 2:21, 2:24, 2:25, Revelation 22:11.

End Notes

1. Berkhof, Louis. *Systematic Theology.* Wm. B. Eerdmans Publishing Co., Grand Rapids, MI, 1996, page 280.
2. www.unicefusa.org.
3. John Paul II. *The Gospel of Life.* Times Books, Evangelium Vitae, 1995, 115–122.
4. Bernard of Clairvaux. Abridged, edited, and introduced by Houston, James M. *The Love of God and Spiritual Friendship.* Multnomah Press, Portland, OR, 1983, pages 7–8.

CHAPTER ELEVEN

Rest and Determination

When we lose our sense of who we are, why we are, and what our purpose is as human beings, our lives lose congruency, integrity. We literally become sick because all health, all life, flows from I AM, the three in one. If you look around, you can see we all are broken and in need. Everyone is seeking peace and rest at a breakneck speed.

On a recent trip to my office three miles away from my house in a small university town of fifty thousand people, I took note of the anxiety of that brief journey of only about ten minutes. After pulling out from my relatively short street, which is two blocks long with a cul-de-sac at one end, I tried to move from that quiet onto the main artery. The traffic was moving at more than forty-five miles per hour on a street marked at a thirty-mile per hour traffic zone. I waited for enough time to jump into the flow without making the person I pulled in front of too angry. I accelerated as fast as I could in order to get in line.

Who knew you would need a car that went from zero to fifty within five seconds to travel small-town streets? I drive a little Toyota, not a Porsche! Traveling along, the young woman behind me was so close to my rear window I could read her lips as she had one hand to her ear holding her cell phone, that is, if I could read lips. I am pretty sure she was agitated about something, though, as fast as she was talking.

As I pulled up to the stop sign, I wondered if she would actually stop as she got even closer to my back window when I slowed down. Keeping my eye on her and watching the road in front, I had to stop short as the person turning across in front of me cut a line across the corner, clearing a big swath through my lane. Luckily the woman behind me stopped in time not to crunch my bumper from behind.

As we traveled on, the car behind me gave me a little room to breathe as she made an attempt to look like she was going to stop for the stop sign also. Whew! She wasn't so close. No, oh, not for long. There she was again, so close I could see her glancing back anxiously as she tried to continue her conversation. I saw the man behind her was as close, maybe closer, tailing her car. As I began to come to the corner where I turn off the main artery, I turned on my signal light. I tried to slow down. I couldn't slow down too much because she kept getting closer and closer. I took the corner at a speed far greater than I was comfortable with. The line of cars speeded past. Whew! What a ten-minute trip!

Bernard of Clairvaux writes, "Every rational person naturally desires to be always satisfied with what it esteems to be preferable. It is never satisfied with something which lacks the qualities it desires to have. So if a man has chosen a wife because of her beauty, then he will look out with a roving eye for more beautiful women. Or if he is desirous of being well dressed he will look out for even more expensive clothes. No matter how rich he is, if wealth is his desire, he will envy those who are richer than he is ...

"Likewise, men in high places are drawn are drawn on by insatiable ambitions to climb higher and higher still. Indeed there is no end to all this because unsatisfied desires have no final satisfaction if they cannot be defined as absolutely the best or highest.

"Need we wonder that a man cannot find contentment with what is less or worse since he seeks peace and satisfaction in what is highest and best? So how stupid and mad it is to seek to find peace or satisfaction in that which cannot fulfill these needs. So no matter how many things one possesses, he will always be lusting for what is perceived to be still missing. Discontented, he will spend himself in restlessness and futility. Thus the restless heart runs to and fro looking for the pleasures of this life in weariness of the evanescent and the unreal. He is like a starving man who thinks anything he can stuff down his throat is not enough, for his eyes are still looking at what he has not eaten. Thus man craves continually for what is still lacking, with more anxiety in his preoccupation with what he lacks rather than having any joy or contentment in what he has already got ...

"Yet foolishly they reject what would lead them to their true goal which is found not in consumption but in consummation. So they wear themselves out in futility without reaching their blessed consummation because they stake their happiness on earthly things instead of upon their Creator. They seek to try each one in turn rather than to think of coming to Him who is Lord of all the universe.

"Suppose, even if they could succeed in the realization of their longings, so they possessed the whole world (Matthew 16:26). Yet without having God who is the Author of all being, then the same principle that makes them restless for more would still leave then dissatisfied.

"Only God can give them that ultimate satisfaction."[1]

It is no wonder we are anxious—life whizzes by awfully fast. We all experience anxiety, become overstressed, and sometimes become overwhelmed by just day-to-day life. Some experience deeper anxiety and lose their ability to cope in a healthy manner.

According to the *Baker Encyclopedia of Psychology*, about 4 percent of people suffer from some type of anxiety disorder. A particularly disruptive disorder that is normally brought on by very severe distress is post-traumatic stress disorder. Severe stressful situations include atrocities in war, rape, witnessing murder, and being abused or tortured. Psychologists find the commonality of events that bring on PTSD are that they are not common experiences; they are profoundly intense and severe and they involve a strong potential for physical harm.[2] With all the strife and discord in the world, it is a wonder that we are not all more anxious than what we appear on the outside to be. The absolute love of I AM, the three in one, though, permeates life. None of us would even be still here without love being poured out to all. I AM is overflowing with steadfast love that reaches to even those who hate Him. This kind of love is an important part of imaging forth His glory.

> Matthew 5:43–48: You have heard that it was said, "You shall love your neighbor and hate your enemy." But I say to you, love your enemies and pray for those who persecute you, so that you may be sons of your Father who is in heaven. For he makes his sun rise on the evil and on the good, and sends rain on the just and on the unjust. For if you love those who love you, what reward do you have? Do not even the tax collectors do the same? And if you greet only your brothers, what more are you doing than others? Do not even the Gentiles do the same? You therefore must be perfect, as your heavenly Father is perfect.

Complete, perfect, absolute love does not love because love is deserved. Love flows from within in spite of any barriers to love from without.

I have been researching to see if there was ever a prolonged period on earth when there was not a war being fought. It seems there have been recorded wars all the way back five thousand years where some societal group or nation was trying to dominate by force another group or nation. The first sets of brothers were the first people to compete and had the desire to dominate and even kill each other. Nightmares, reliving the stressful event, lapses from reality, illusions, and other interferences in cognitive congruence are some of the symptoms experienced in PTSD. There are other forms of anxiety disorders that bring on different painful or disruptive symptoms, however the point is that being overstressed can cause both physically harmful and emotionally disruptive effects. Not many of us experience stress-related effects to this degree, but for many people around us stress-induced insomnia, depression, or anxiety is at least mildly disruptive.

I AM, the three in one, is the means to and provider of rest. Isa, Al-Masih, Jesus, Yeshua, said (Matthew 11:28-30), "Come to me, all who labor and are heavy laden, and I will give you rest. Take my yoke upon you, and learn from me, for I am gentle and lowly in heart, and you will find rest for your souls. For my yoke is easy, and my burden is light."

John Piper writes, "First, notice that all conditions are summed up in love. Paul said, concerning doing good and obeying God's commandments, that this is precisely what love does. Love does no wrong to a neighbor, therefore love is the fulfillment of the law" (Romans 13:5). Forgiveness is clearly an expression of love (1 Corinthians 13:5). Paul also says that love is the essence of holiness or sanctification: "May the Lord cause you to increase and abound in love ... so that he may establish your hearts ... in holiness" (1 Thessalonians 3:12–13). In other words, all the behavior that is required of a Christian may be summed up in love. "Let all that you do be done in love" (1 Corinthians 16:14).

"What we have seen then is that the ten conditions of future grace ... are all summed up in faith. And the behavioral conditions we have just discussed are all summed up in love. Which means we may now say the conditions a Christian must meet, to go on enjoying the blessings of future grace, are faith and love."[3]

Rest was instituted by I AM and in the beginning a pattern was set up through creation of creativity and rest. Genesis 2:2–3: "And on the seventh day God finished his work that he had done, and he rested on the seventh day from all his work that he had done. So God blessed the seventh day and made it holy, because on it God rested from all his work that he had done in creation."

The pattern of creation and rest is highlighted throughout the history of followers of I AM. A servant purchased for work in a household was to be set free for no price on the seventh year of service (Exodus 21:2). Land that produced crops was to be worked for six years but every seventh year was not to be harvested; the land was to rest. The ebb and flow of creativity was to be observed weekly; one out of seven days was a day of rest and renewal through concentrated focus on I AM. Annually one out of every seven months was to be observed as rest and one out of every seven years was to be observed as rest. Rest was to benefit all. Exodus 23:6–12: "You shall not pervert the justice due to your poor in his lawsuit. Keep far from a false charge, and do not kill the innocent and righteous, for I will not acquit the wicked. And you shall take no bribe, for a bribe blinds the clear-sighted and subverts the cause of those who are in the right. You shall not oppress a sojourner. You know the heart of a sojourner, for you were sojourners in the land of Egypt. For six years you shall sow your land and gather in its yield, but the seventh year you shall let it rest and lie fallow, that the poor of your people may eat; and what they leave the beasts of the field may eat. You shall do likewise with your vineyard, and with your olive orchard. Six days you shall do your work, but on the seventh day you shall rest; that your ox and your donkey may have rest, and the son of your servant woman, and the alien, may be refreshed."

The loving character of I AM, the three in one, is to be reflected to all through the days and seasons of rest and creativity. Rest is to be observed as a time to focus on I AM. Resting is to reflect on the ultimate rest from sin and sadness that will come for all who look to I AM and rest in Him for comfort and solace.

> Hebrews 3:15–4:11: As it is said, "Today, if you hear his voice, do not harden your hearts as in the rebellion." For who were those who heard and yet rebelled? Was it not all those who left Egypt led by Moses? And with whom was he provoked for forty years? Was it not with those who sinned, whose bodies fell in the wilderness? And to whom did he swear that they would not enter his rest, but to those who were disobedient? So we see that they were unable to enter because of unbelief. Therefore, while the promise of entering his rest still stands, let us fear lest any of you should seem to have failed to reach it. For good news came to us just as to them, but the message they heard did not benefit them, because they were not united by faith with those who listened. For we who have believed enter that rest, as he has said, "As I swore in my wrath, 'They shall not enter my rest,'" although his

works were finished from the foundation of the world. For he has somewhere spoken of the seventh day in this way: "And God rested on the seventh day from all his works." And again in this passage he said, "They shall not enter my rest." Since therefore it remains for some to enter it, and those who formerly received the good news failed to enter because of disobedience, again he appoints a certain day, "Today," saying through David so long afterward, in the words already quoted, "Today, if you hear his voice, do not harden your hearts." For if Joshua had given them rest, God would not have spoken of another day later on. So then, there remains a Sabbath rest for the people of God, for whoever has entered God's rest has also rested from his works as God did from his. Let us therefore strive to enter that rest, so that no one may fall by the same sort of disobedience.

In a different manner, the lack of enough stimuli, activity, or stress can also be harmful in many ways. In fact, physical and mental activities that provide adequate stress to body and mind are necessary for health. Without physical exercise and mental stimuli, our bodies and our brains diminish in capacity. Exercise stimulates capacity for both the body and brain. It increases blood circulation and oxygen supplies, which enhance energy and waste removal.

According to the Franklin Institute, exercise can be observed to increase cerebral blood vessels, improve memory skills, concentration, and abstract reasoning. Studies have shown that exercise contributes to new brain cell growth. Inactive individuals were twice as likely to develop Alzheimer's disease or dementia. Similar studies have also shown that exercise is just as effective as medication in treating major depression. The ebb and flow of exercise and rest are essential parts of health, yet it is worthy to note that rest does not necessarily mean inactivity. It can be restful and relaxing to go on a hike, take a bicycle ride, or walk the dogs around the neighborhood. In fact, exercise releases chemicals that cause feelings of well-being and calm that allow us to be more creative and productive.[4]

There is a reason that creative activity is emphasized to us in a ratio of six to one in relation to rest. It may well be that the creativity of imaging forth I AM through the productive activity of work, if focused on working through the power He supplies, is the most effective way to become more creatively loving. Rest in a different way refocuses us on Him as the power supply so that we can continue to be more and more productive through His empowerment. 1 Peter 4:7–11: "The end of all things is at hand; therefore be self-controlled and sober-minded for the sake of your prayers. Above all, keep loving one another earnestly, since love covers a multitude of sins. Show hospitality to one another without grumbling. As each has received a gift, use it to serve one another, as good stewards of God's varied grace: whoever speaks, as one who speaks oracles of God; whoever serves, as one who serves by the strength that God supplies—in order that in everything God may be glorified through Jesus Christ. To him belong glory and dominion forever and ever. Amen."

In regard to the contribution of both rest and determination, Anthony Hoekema says, "No protestant creed has a better or more complete statement of the doctrine of the perseverance of true believers than the Canons of Dordt (1618–19) ...

"After the first two articles ... have described the inclination of believers to fall into daily sins of weakness, Article 3 states that the converted, if left to their own resources, would not be able to remain standing in the grace of God. 'But,' the article continues, 'God is faithful, mercifully strengthening them in the grace once conferred on them and powerfully preserving them in it to the end.'

"Article 4 goes on to indicate that true believers may indeed fall into serious sins if they fail to watch and pray. But article 6 affirms that: 'God, who is rich in mercy according to his unchangeable purpose of election does not take his Holy Spirit from his own completely, even when they fall grievously. Neither does he let them fall down so far that they forfeit the grace of adoption and the state of justification, or commit the sin which leads to death(the sin against the Holy Spirit), and plunge themselves, entirely forsaken by him, into eternal ruin.'

"In Article 7 the Canons maintain that God will by his Word and Spirit certainly and effectually renew to repentance those of his people who have fallen into serious sins. Then follows Article 8, which underscores the fact that the preservation of God's people is due entirely to God's grace: 'So it is not by their own merits or strength but by God's undeserved mercy that they (true believers) neither forfeit faith and grace totally nor remain in their own downfalls to the end and are lost. With respect to themselves this not only easily could happen, but also undoubtedly would happen; but with respect to God it cannot possibly happen, since his plan cannot be changed, his promise cannot fail, the calling according to his purpose cannot be revoked, the merit of Christ as well as his interceding and preserving cannot be nullified, and the sealing of the Holy Spirit can neither be invalidated nor wiped out.' It would be hard to compose a more beautiful statement of this doctrine. Once again the thought is repeated that the perseverance of true believers is due not to their merits or strength but only to God's undeserved mercy. And once again the real heartbeat of this doctrine comes home to us: God's unchanging faithfulness to his promises. This is what we lean on-weak, changeable, and fickle sinners that we are—when we profess to believe in the perseverance of God's true people.

"It should further be observed, however, that the Canons of Dordt do not in any way support the erroneous understanding of this doctrine that some seem to have: namely, 'Once saved, always saved, regardless of how we live.' Articles 12 and 13 make clear that the assurance of our preservation by God, far from being an occasion for carelessness in living or in morals, is actually an incentive to godliness: 'The assurance of perseverance, however, so far from making true believers proud and carnally self-assured, is rather the true root of humility, of childlike respect, of genuine godliness, of endurance in every conflict, of fervent prayers, of steadfastness in cross bearing and in confessing the truth, and of well-founded joy in God. Reflecting on this benefit provides an incentive to a serious and continual practice of thanksgiving and good works, as is evident from the testimonies of Scripture and the examples of the saints.

"Neither does the renewed confidence of perseverance produce immorality or lack of concern for godliness in those put back on their feet after a fall, but it produces a much greater concern to observe carefully the ways of the Lord which he prepared in advance."

"The teaching of the perseverance of true believers is one of the most comforting teachings of Scripture. We learn from it that God by his power keeps his people from falling away from him, that Christ will never permit anyone to snatch them out of his hand, and that the Holy Spirit seals them for the day of redemption. Our heavenly Father holds us securely in his grasp, that is our ultimate comfort in life and death. We rest finally not in our hold of God but on God's hold of us.

"Yet this teaching also urges us to persevere in the faith- and this is our challenge. We can only persevere through God's strength and by his grace. But to teach this doctrine in such a way as to present only its comfort and not its challenge, only the security and not the exhortation, is to teach it one-sidedly. And the Bible constantly warns us against such one sidedness ...

"The doctrine of the perseverance of true believers, therefore, is both a comfort and a challenge. But the challenge is based on the comfort. We can be certain that we shall persevere to the end only because God has promised to enable us to do so. And so we rest in him, for time and eternity, knowing that he will never let us go."[5]

I AM, the three in one, is eternally active yet always at rest. He is constantly ruling, supplying, creating, recreating, and yet never is tired. He is always described as sitting yet he is never inactive. I have heard it said that He is never in a hurry, but He is always on time. It is striking how His steadfast love is associated with strength. Psalm 59:16–17: "But I will sing of your strength; I will sing aloud of your steadfast love in the morning. For you have been to me a fortress and a refuge in the day of my distress. O my Strength I will sing praises to you, for you, O God, are my fortress, the God who shows me steadfast love."

It is in and by His strength that we are empowered and renewed as we rest in Him and wait for His strength. Isaiah 40:28–31: "Have you not known? Have you not heard? The LORD is the everlasting God, the Creator of the ends of the earth. He does not faint or grow weary; his understanding is unsearchable. He gives power to the faint, and to him who has no might he increases strength. Even youths shall faint and be weary, and young men shall fall exhausted; but they who wait for the LORD shall renew their strength; they shall mount up with wings like eagles; they shall run and not be weary; they shall walk and not faint."

However waiting and resting are not the same as inactivity.

> 2 Peter 1:2–10: May grace and peace be multiplied to you in the knowledge of God and of Jesus our Lord. His divine power has granted to us all things that pertain to life and godliness, through the knowledge of him who called us to his own glory and excellence, by which he has granted to us his precious and very great promises, so that through them you may become partakers of the divine nature, having escaped from the corruption that is in the world because of sinful desire. For this very reason, make every effort to supplement your faith with virtue, and virtue with knowledge, and knowledge with self-control, and self-control with steadfastness, and steadfastness with godliness, and godliness with brotherly affection, and brotherly affection with love. For if these qualities are yours and are increasing, they keep you from being ineffective or unfruitful in the knowledge of our Lord Jesus Christ. For whoever lacks these qualities is so nearsighted that he is blind, having forgotten that he was cleansed from his former sins. Therefore, brothers, be all the more diligent to make your calling and election sure, for if you practice these qualities you will never fall.

Rest is the characteristic of believing that gives us the ability see past obstacles to our own well-being and the well-being of others so that we can peacefully work to overcome those obstacles and overthrow those who are setting them up.

Determination is the characteristic of believing that gives us the ability to persist until that which has been started is completed.

Shabat (rest, cease, desist, be completed, remove, exterminate, destroy.) Genesis 2:2, 2:3, 8:22, Exodus 5:5, 12:15, 16:30, 23:12, 31:17, 34:21, Leviticus 2:13, 23:32, 26:6, 26:34, 26:35, Deuteronomy 32:26, Joshua 5:12, 22:25, Ruth 4:14, 2 Kings 23:5, 23:11, 2 Chronicles 16:5, 36:21, Nehemiah 4:11, 6:3, 32:1, Psalm 8:2, 46:9, 89:44, 119:119, Proverbs 18:18, 22:10, Isaiah 13:11, 14:4, 16:10, 17:3, 21:2, 24:8, 30:7, 30:11, 33:8, Jeremiah 7:34, 16:9, 31:36, 36:29, 48:33, 48:35, Lamentations 5:14, 5:15, Ezekiel 6:6, 7:24, 12:23, 16:41, 23:27, 23:48, 26:13, 30:10, 30:13, 30:18, 33:28, 34:10, 34:25, Daniel 9:27, 11:18 ,Hosea 1:4, 2:11, 7:4, Amos 8:4, **Shabbaton** Exodus 16:23, 31:15, 35:2, **Leviticus 16:31,** 23:3, 23:24, 23:32, 23:39, 25:4, 25:5.

Shalom (peacefulness, wholeness, completeness, soundness, welfare, health, prosperity, wellness, tranquility, contentment.) Genesis 15:15, 26:29, 26:31, 28:21, 29:6 ,37:4, 37:14, 41:16, 43:23, 43:27, 43:28, 44:17, Exodus 4:18, 18:7, 18:23, Leviticus 26:6, **Numbers 6:26,** 25:12, Deuteronomy 2:26, 20:10, 20:11, 23:6, 29:19, Joshua 9:15, 10:21, Judges 4:17, 6:23, 8:9, 11:13, 11:31, 18:6, 18:15 19:20, 21:13, 1 Samuel 1:17, 7:14, 10:4, 16:4, 17:18, 17:22, 20:7, 20:13, 20:21, 20:42, 25:5, 25:6, 25:35, 29:7, 30:21, 2 Samuel 3:21, 3:22, 3:23, 8:10, 11:7, 15:9, 15:27, 17:3, 18:28, 18:29, 18:32, 19:24, 19:30, 20:9, 1 Kings 2:5, 2:6, 2:13, 2:33, 4:24, 5:12, 20:18, 22:17, 22:27, 22:28, 2 Kings 4:23, 4:26, 5:19, 5:21, 5:22, 9:11, 9:17, 9:18, 9:19, 9:22, 9:31, 10:13, 20:19, 22:20, 1 Chronicles 12:17, 12:18, 18:10, 22:9, 2 Chronicles 15:5, 18:16, 18:26, 18:27, 19:1 ,34:28, Ezra 9:12, Esther 2:11, 9:30, 10:3, Job 5:24, 15:21, 21:9, 25:2, **Psalm 4:8,** 28:3, 29:11, 34:14, 35:20, **35:27, 37:11, 37:37,** 38:3, 41:9, 55:18, 55:20, 69:22, 72:3, 72:7, 73:3, **85:8, 85:10, 119:165,** 120:6, 120:7, 122:6, 122:7, 122:8, 125:5, 128:6, 147:14,

Proverbs 3:2, 3:17, 12:20, Ecclesiastes 3:8, Song 8:10, **Isaiah 9:6, 9:7, 26:3, 26:12, 27:5, 32:17, 32:18, 33:**7, 38:17, 39:8, 41:3, **45:7, 48:18, 48:22, 52:**7, **53:5, 54:**10, 54:13, 55:12, 57:2, 57:19, 57:21, 59:8, 60:17, 66:12, Jeremiah 4:10, 6:14, 8:11, 8:15, 9:8, 12:5, 12:12, 13:19, 14:13, 14:19, 15:5, 16:5, 20:10, 23:17, 25:37, 28:9, **29:7, 29:11,** 30:5, **33:6, 33:**9, 34:5, 38:4, 38:22, 43:12, Lamentations 3:17, Ezekiel 7:25, 13:10, 13:16, 34:25, 37:26, Daniel 10:19, Oba 1:7, Micah 3:5, 5:5, Nahum 1:15, Haggai 2:9, Zechariah 6:13, 8:10, 8:12, 8:16, 8:19, 9:10, Malachi 2:5, 2:6 **Shalem Genesis 14:18,** 15:16, 33:18, 34:21, Deuteronomy 25:15, 27:6, Joshua 8:31, Ruth 2:12, 1 Kings 6:7, 8:61, 11:4, 15:3, 15:14, 2 Kings 20:3, 1 Chronicles 12:38, 28:19 ,29:9, 29:19, 2 Chronicles 8:16, 15:17, **16:9,** 19:9, 25:2, Psalm 76:2, Proverbs 11:1, Isaiah 38:3, Amos 1:6, 1:9, Nahum 1:12.

Anapauo (rest, stop, cease, refresh, remain quiet, revive.) **Matthew 11:28,** 26:45, Mark 6:31, 14:41, Luke 12:19, 1 Corinthians 16:18, 2 Corinthians 7:13, Phile 1:7, 1:20, 1 Peter 4:14, **Revelation 6:11, 14:13, Anapausis, Matthew 11:29,** 12:43, Luke 11:24, Revelation 4:8, 14:11, **Epanapauomai,** Luke 10:6, Romans 2:17, **Sunanapauomai,** Romans 15:32.

Katapausis Acts 7:49, **Hebrews 3:11, 3:18, 4:1, 4:3, 4:5, 4:10, 4:11.**

Teleios(completed, whole, perfected, finished, accomplished, performed, fulfilled, kept, concluded, reached the goal) **Matthew 5:48,** 19:21, Romans 12:2, 1 Corinthians 2:6, **13:10,** 14:20, **Ephesians 4:13,** Phil 3:15, Colossians 1:28, 4:12, Hebrews 5:14, 9:11, **James 1:4, 1:17, 1:25, 3:**2, 1 **Peter 1:13, 1 John 4:18 Teleiotes Colossians 3:14,** Hebrews 6:1, **12:2 Teleo** Matthew 10:23, 11:1, 13:53, 17:24, 19:1, 26:1, Luke 2:39, 12:50, **18:31,** 22:37, John 19:28, 19:30, Acts 13:29, Romans 2:27, 13:6, Galatians 5:16, **2 Timothy 4:7,** Hebrews 2:10, 9:9, 10:1, **James 2:8,** Revelation 10:7, 11:7, 15:1, 15:8, 17:17, 20:3, 20:5, 20:7 **Epiteleo,** Luke 13:32, Romans 15:28, 2 **Corinthians 7:1,** 8:6, 8:11, **Galatians 3:3, Phil 1:6,** Hebrews 8:5, 9:6, 1 Peter 5:9.

Irene(peace, quietness, set at one again) Matthew 10:13, 10:34 Mark 5:34; Luke 1:79;2:14, 29;7:50;8:48;10:5, 6;11:21;12:51;14:32, 19:38,

42;24:36 John 14:27;16:33;20:19, 21, 26 Acts 7:26;9:31;10:36;12:20;15:3 3;16:36; 24:2 Romans 1:7;2:10;3:17;5:1;8:6;10:15;14:17, 19;15:13, 33;16:20 1 Corinthians 1:3;7:15;14:33; 16:11 2 Corinthians 1:2;13:11 Galatians 1:3;5:22;6:16 Ephesians 1:2;2:14, 15, 17;4:3;6:15, 23 Phil 1:2;4:7, 9 Col 1:2;3:15 1 Thessalonians 1:1;5:3, 23 2 Thessalonians 1:2;3:16, 1 Timothy 1:2 2 Timothy 1:2;2:22 Titus 1:4, Phile 1:3 Hebrews 7:2;11:31;12:14;13:20 James 2:16;3:18 1 Peter 1:2;3:11;5:14 2 Peter 1:2;3:14 2 John 1:3 3 John 1:14 Jude 1:2 Revelation 1:4; 6:4.

Cun (determined, steadfast, be firm, be established, put right, correct, stable, secure, ready, prepared, ordered, upright, honest) Genesis 41:32, 43:16, 43:25, Exodus 8:26, **15:17,** 16:5, 19:11, 19:15, 23:20, 34:2, Numbers 21:27, 23:1, 23:29, Deuteronomy 13:14, 17:4, 19:3, 32:6, Joshua 1:11, 3:17, 4:3, 4:4, 8:4, Judges 12:6, 16:26, 16:29, 1 Samuel 7:3, 13:13, 20:31, 23:22, 23:23, 26:4, 2 Samuel 5:12, **7:12, 7:13, 7:16, 7:24, 7:26,** 1 Kings 2:12, 2:24, 2:45, 2:46, 5:18, 6:19, 1 Chronicles 9:32, 12:39, 14:2, 15:1, 15:3, 15:12, 16:30, 17:11, 17:12, 17:1, 17:24, 18:8, 22:3, 22:5, 22:10, 22:14, 28:2, 28:7, 29:2, 29:3, 29:16, 29:18, 29:19, 2 Chronicles 1:4, 2:7, 2:9, 3:1, 8:16, 12:1, 12:14, 17:5, 19:3, 20:33, 26:14, 27:6, 29:19, 29:35, 29:36, 30:19, 31:11, 35:4, 35:6, 35:10, 35:14, 35:15, 35:16, 35:20, Ezra 3:3, 7:10, Nehemiah 8:10, Esther 6:4, 7:10, Job 8:8, 11:13, 12:5, 15:23, 15:35, 18:12, 21:8, 27:16, 27:17, 28:27, 29:7, 31:15, 38:41, 42:7, 42:8, Psalm 5:9, 7:9, 7:12, 7:13, 8:3, 9:7, **10:17,** 11:2, 21:12, 24:2, **37:23,** 38:17, 40:2, 48:8, **51:10, 57:6, 57:7,** 59:4, 65:6, 65:9, 68:9, 68:10, 74:16, **78:8, 78:20, 78:37, 89:2, 89:4, 89:21, 89:37,** 90:17, 93:,93:2, 96:10, 99:4, **101:7,** 102:28, 103:19, 107:36, 108:1, 112:7, **119:5, 119:73, 119:90, 119:133,** 140:11, 141:2, 147:8, Proverbs 3:19, **4:18, 4:26, 6:**8, 8:27, **12:3, 12:19, 16:3, 16:9, 16:12,** 19:29, 20:18, 21:29, 21:31, 22:18, 24:3, 24:27, 25:5, 29:14, 30:25, Isaiah 2:2, 9:7, 14:21, **16:5,** 30:33, 40:20, 45:18, 51:13, **54:14,** 62:7, **Jeremiah 10:12, 10:23,** 30:20, 33:2, 46:14, 51:12, 51:15, Ezekiel 4:3, 4:7, 7:14, 16:7, 28:13, 38:7, 40:43, 43:25, 45:17, 45:22, 45:23, 45:24, 46:2, 46:7, 46:12, 46:13, 46:14, 46:15, Hosea 6:3, Amos 4:12, Micah 4:1, Nahum 2:3, 2:5, Habakkuk 2:12, Zephaniah 1:7, Zechariah 5:11.

Meno (determined, steadfast, continue, abide, persist, remain, persevere, lasting, permanent.) Matthew 10:11, 11:23, 26:38, Mark 6:10, 14:34, Luke 1:56, 8:27, 9:4, 10:7, 19:5, 24:29, John 1:32, 1:33, 1:38, 1:39, 2:12, 3:36, 4:40, **5:38, 6:27, 6:56,** 7:9, **8:31, 8:35,** 9:41, 10:40, 11:6, 12:24, 12:34, 12:46, 14:10, 14:16, 14:17, 14:25, **15:4, 15:5, 15:6, 15:7, 15:9, 15:10, 15:11, 15:16,** 19:31, 21:22, Acts 5:4, 9:43, 16:15, 18:3, 18:20, 20:5, 20:15, 20:23, 21:7, 21:8, 27:31, 27:41, 28:16, 28:30, Romans 9:11, 1 Corinthians 3:14, 7:8, 7:11, 7:20, 7:24, 7:40, **13:13,** 15:6, 2 Corinthians 3:11, 3:14, 9:9, **Phil 1:25,** 1 Timothy 2:15, 2 Timothy 2:13, **3:14,** 4:20, **Hebrews 7:3, 7:24,** 10:34, 12:27, 13:1, 13:14, 1 Peter 1:23, 1:25, **1 John 2:6, 2:10, 2:14, 2:17, 2:19, 2:24, 2:27, 3:6, 3:9, 3:14, 3:15, 3:17, 3:24, 4:12, 4:13, 4:15, 4:16,** 2 John 1:2, 1:9, Revelation 17:10.

Epimeno John 8:7, Acts 10:48, 12:16, 13:43, **15:34,** 21:4, 21:10, 28:12, 28:14, Romans 6:1, **11:22, 11:23, 1** Corinthians 16:7, 16:8, Galatians 1:18, Phil 1:24, **Colossians 1:23, 1 Timothy 4:16 Hupomeno Matthew 10:22, 24:13, Mark 13:13,** Luke 2:43, Acts 17:14, Romans 12:12, 1 **Corinthians 13:7, 2 Timothy 2:10, 2:12, Hebrews 10:32, 12:2, 12:3, 12:7, James 1:12,** 5:11, 1 Peter 2:20 **Hupomone** Luke 8:15, 21:19, Romans 2:7, 5:3, 5:4, 8:25, **15:4, 15:5, 2** Corinthians 1:6, 6:4, 12:12, Colossians 1:11, 1 Thessalonians 1:3, 2 Thessalonians 1:4, 3:5, 1 Timothy 6:11, 2 Timothy 3:10, Titus 2:2, **Hebrews 10:36, 12:1, James 1:3, 1:4, 5:11,** 2 Peter 1:6, Revelation 1:9, 2:2, 2:3, 2:19, 3:10, 13:10, 14:12.

End Notes

1. Bernard of Clairvaux. Abridged, edited, and introduced by Houston, James M. *The Love of God and Spiritual Friendship.* Multnomah Press, Portland, OR, 1983, pages 149–151.
2. Benner, David G., ed. *Baker Encyclopedia of Psychology.* Baker Book House, Grand Rapids, MI, 1985, pages 857–858.
3. Piper, Dr. John. *Future Grace,* Multnomah Books, Sisters, OR, 1995, page 254.
4. The Franklin Institute. www.fi.edu/brainexercise.
5. Hoekema, Anthony H. *Saved by Grace.* Wm. B. Eerdmans Publishing, Grand Rapids, MI, 1989, pages 253–254.

CHAPTER TWELVE

Love Never Fails

Our world, earth, and its inhabitants have, from creation, been racing toward a beginning. I AM, the three in one, has planned from before the creation of the world a perfect world, a world of fullness and fulfillment. God planned a world where absolute love will transform those who love I AM here and now by His overflowing, steadfast, loving kindness because they will keep their eyes on him and not look away. We will love Him and He will transform us by His love. 1 Corinthians 13:12: "For now we see in a mirror dimly, but then face to face. Now I know in part; then I shall know fully, even as I have been fully known." When He returns, we will become like Him in His love. 1 John 3:2- 3: "Beloved, we are God's children now, and what we will be has not yet appeared; but we know that when he appears we shall be like him, because we shall see him as he is." And everyone who thus hopes in him purifies himself as he is pure."

The race is a dangerous one filled with lots of land mines and enemy attacks. The difference between mankind and the rest of creation, according to Daniel Gilbert, is "The human being is the only animal that thinks about the future."[1] We are wired to look forward and in looking forward to look for happiness, fulfillment, yes, love.

John Piper writes, "The safest place in the universe is with our arms around the neck of God. And the most dangerous place is any path where we flee from his presence."[2] I AM is the place of beginning and He is the beginning of culmination, of completion, where perfect, absolute love casts out all fear. I AM has declared (Jeremiah 29:11), "For I know the plans I have for you, declares the LORD, plans for welfare and not for evil, to give you a future and a hope."

David F. Wells says, "The Christian confession, as we have seen, is that this future has already arrived, that it has been realized in ways more grand than could have been imagined, that it was divinely ushered in through Christ's death, and that it can be experienced and tasted now, thereby transforming human life. For those in Christ, "the old has passed away, behold, the new has come" (II Cor. 5:37). This is not simply a personal statement, that at a certain time their conversion happened. It is even more profound than that. It is Paul's affirmation that those in Christ have already entered the age to come and have been extracted from the world of darkness in which they once were at ease and at home.

"Christian hope is not about wishing that things will get better, that somehow emptiness will go away, meaning will return, and life will be stripped of its uncertainties, its psychological aches, and anxieties. Nor does it have anything to do with techniques for improving fallen human life, be those therapeutic or even religious. Hope, instead, has to do, biblically speaking, with the knowledge that "the age to come" is already penetrating "this age," that sin, death, and meaninglessness of the one is being transformed by the righteousness, life, and meaning of the other, that what has emptied out life, what has scarred and blackened it, is being displaced by what is rejuvenating and transforming it. More than that, hope is hope because it knows it has become part of a realm, a kingdom, which endures, where evil is doomed and will be banished ..."[3]

The world planned would not have death, crying, or pain. In this world we live in now there will be pain, heartache, and troubles unending. John 16:33, "I have said these things to you, that in me you may have peace. In the world you will have tribulation. But take heart; I have overcome the world."

In the world being made new, there will be no death.

1 Corinthians 15:20-28: But in fact Christ has been raised from the dead, the first fruits of those who have fallen asleep. For as by a man came death, by a man has come also the resurrection of the dead. For as in Adam all die, so also in Christ shall all be made alive. But each in his own order: Christ the first fruits, then at his coming those who belong to Christ. Then comes the end, when he delivers the kingdom to God the Father after destroying every rule and every authority and power. For he must reign until he has put all his enemies under his feet. The last enemy to be destroyed is death. For "God has put all things in subjection under his feet." But when it says, "all things are put in subjection," it is plain that he is excepted who put all things in subjection under him. When all things are subjected to him, then the Son himself will also be subjected to him who put all things in subjection under him, that God may be all in all.

I AM, the three in one, is overflowing with love, grace, and mercy. His kingdom of love has broken into this world in Jesus of Nazareth, Yeshua the Messiah, Isa Al-Masih. His sacrificial death has destroyed the power of death, redeeming those who have, do now, and will love Him. His resurrection from the dead has vindicated the just nature of His mercy and forgiveness as well as the justice of His anger against those who have, do now and will reject His love. The barrier between I AM and mankind was torn down. His love, life, humanity, deity, death, resurrection and ascension was attested to by many and has been proclaimed throughout the world by faithful followers. Matthew 27:51-53: "And behold, the curtain of the temple was torn in two, from top to bottom. And the earth shook, and the rocks were split. The tombs also were opened. And many bodies of the saints who had fallen asleep were raised, and coming out of the tombs after his resurrection they went into the holy city and appeared to many."

So death is swallowed up in loving sacrifice and what we will be has begun in us in this world.

> 1 Corinthians 15:49–57: Just as we have borne the image of the man of dust, we shall also bear the image of the man of heaven. I tell you this, brothers: flesh and blood cannot inherit the kingdom of God, nor does the perishable inherit the imperishable. Behold! I tell you a mystery. We shall not all sleep, but we shall all be changed, in a moment, in the twinkling of an eye, at the last trumpet. For the trumpet will sound, and the dead will be raised imperishable, and we shall be changed. For this perishable body must put on the imperishable, and this mortal body must put on immortality. When the perishable puts on the imperishable, and the mortal puts on immortality, then shall come to pass the saying that is written: "Death is swallowed up in victory. "O death, where is your victory? O death, where is your sting?" The sting of death is sin, and the power of sin is the law. But thanks be to God, who gives us the victory through our Lord Jesus Christ.

This present world of fear and danger then is not the world planned. John 18:36: "Jesus answered, 'My kingdom is not of this world. If my kingdom were of this world, my servants would have been fighting, that I might not be delivered over to the Jews. But my kingdom is not from the world.'" This world is temporal and fading away. It is not something to cling to I AM is returning and His gracious patience and forgiveness toward us will have an end.

> 2 Peter 3:5–14: For they deliberately overlook this fact, that the heavens existed long ago, and the earth was formed out of water and through water by the word of God, and that by means of these the world that then

existed was deluged with water and perished. But by the same word the heavens and earth that now exist are stored up for fire, being kept until the day of judgment and destruction of the ungodly. But do not overlook this one fact, beloved, that with the Lord one day is as a thousand years, and a thousand years as one day. The Lord is not slow to fulfill his promise as some count slowness, but is patient toward you, not wishing that any should perish, but that all should reach repentance. But the day of the Lord will come like a thief, and then the heavens will pass away with a roar, and the heavenly bodies will be burned up and dissolved, and the earth and the works that are done on it will be exposed. Since all these things are thus to be dissolved, what sort of people ought you to be in lives of holiness and godliness, waiting for and hastening the coming of the day of God, because of which the heavens will be set on fire and dissolved, and the heavenly bodies will melt as they burn! But according to his promise we are waiting for new heavens and a new earth in which righteousness dwells. Therefore, beloved, since you are waiting for these, be diligent to be found by him without spot or blemish, and at peace.

The allure of the world that is to come is not riches, gold, or precious metals but the wealth of the absolute love of I AM flooding over us and through us to one another.

Revelation 21:1–7: Then I saw a new heaven and a new earth, for the first heaven and the first earth had passed away, and the sea was no more. And I saw the holy city, new Jerusalem, coming down out of heaven from God, prepared as a bride adorned for her husband. And I heard a loud voice from the throne saying, "Behold, the dwelling place of God is with man. He will dwell with them, and they will be his people, and God himself will be with them as their God. He will wipe away every tear from their eyes, and death shall be no more, neither shall there be mourning, nor crying, nor pain anymore, for the former things have passed away." And he who was seated on the throne said, "Behold, I am making all things new." Also he said, "Write this down, for these words are trustworthy and true." And he said to me, "It is done! I am the Alpha and the Omega, the beginning and the end. To the thirsty I will give from the spring of the water of life without payment. The one who conquers will have this heritage, and I will be his God and he will be my son.

Furthermore we are told (Revelation 22:3-5), "No longer will there be anything accursed, but the throne of God and of the Lamb will be in it, and his servants will worship him. They will see his face, and his name will be on their foreheads. And night will be no more. They will need no light of lamp or sun, for the Lord God will be their light, and they will reign forever and ever."

In the interim, this is all being prepared for those who believe.

John 14:1-10: Let not your hearts be troubled. Believe in God; believe also in me. In my Father's house are many rooms. If it were not so, would I have told you that I go to prepare a place for you? And if I go and prepare a place for you, I will come again and will take you to myself, that where I am you may be also. And you know the way to where I am going." Thomas said to him, "Lord, we do not know where you are going. How can we know the way?" Jesus said to him, "I am the way, and the truth, and the life. No one comes to the Father except through me. If you had known me, you would have known my Father also. From now on you do know him and have seen him."

Philip said to him, "Lord, show us the Father, and it is enough for us." Jesus said to him, "Have I been with you so long, and you still do not know me, Philip? Whoever has seen me has seen the Father. How can you say, 'Show us the Father'? Do you not believe that I am in the Father and the Father is in me? The words that I say to you I do not speak on my own authority, but the Father who dwells in me does his works.

These truth's mysteriously have been planned and decided before the foundation of this present world, for I AM is the same yesterday, today, and, yes, forever, and He has known and planned for all possible contingencies to the fulfillment of His loving and absolute purpose and His love never fails.

Matthew 13:35: "This was to fulfill what was spoken by the prophet: 'I will open my mouth in parables; I will utter what has been hidden since the foundation of the world.'" Matthew 25:34: "Then the King will say to those on his right, 'Come, you who are blessed by my Father, inherit the kingdom prepared for you from the foundation of the world.'"

Luke 11:49-50: "Therefore also the Wisdom of God said, 'I will send them prophets and apostles, some of whom they will kill and persecute,' so that the blood of all the prophets, shed from the foundation of the world, may be charged against this generation.'" John 17:24: "Father, I desire that they also, whom you have given me, may be with me where I am, to see my glory that you have given me because you loved me before the foundation of the world."

Ephesians 1:3-6: "Blessed be the God and Father of our Lord Jesus Christ, who has blessed us in Christ with every spiritual blessing in the heavenly places, even as he chose us in him before the foundation of the world, that we should be holy and blameless before him. In love he predestined us for adoption as sons through Jesus Christ, according to the purpose of his will, to the praise of his glorious grace, with which he has blessed us in the Beloved."

Hebrews 4:3: "For we who have believed enter that rest, as he has said, 'As I swore in my wrath, 'They shall not enter my rest,'" although his works were finished from the foundation of the world." Hebrews 9:26–28: "For then he would have had to suffer repeatedly since the foundation of the world. But as it is, he has appeared once for all at the end of the ages to put away sin by the sacrifice of himself. And just as it is appointed for man to die once, and after that comes judgment, Hebrews so Christ, having been offered once to bear the sins of many, will appear a second time, not to deal with sin but to save those who are eagerly waiting for him." 1 Peter 1:20–21: "He was foreknown before the foundation of the world but was made manifest in the last times for the sake of you who through him are believers in God, who raised him from the dead and gave him glory, so that your faith and hope are in God."

This world we live in then is neither a mistake nor a surprise. I AM, the three in one in absolute love, have planned it and will see it to fruition. Rather than create puppets, they have planned to bring about a people who would learn to live loving Him and one another in humility, belief, trust, acceptance, confidence, gratitude, compassion, freedom, stewardship, servanthood, loyalty, purity, justice, rest, and determination. These gifts do not belong to us and are not produced by us. They are gifts given to us as by faith we look to Him.

Adrio Koenig writes, "So it is not at all strange that ... self-manifestation, self-revelation and self-communication of God attain their goal when a person comes to faith.

"Before the proclamation's goal can be broadly outlined, it is necessary to show that this "addition" of faith is no addition at all, and that because of the nature of faith there is agreement ... on the emptiness of faith. This does not mean that faith is unimportant, but rather that its importance—even indispensability—lies in that it is nothing on its own, is not autonomous, is no human contribution, but must receive its content and its meaning from the other side: in fact from God in Christ through the Spirit In faith we confess God as the subject and ourselves as the object of salvation. Salvation means that Christ has fully attained

God's goal for us. And when a person believes this, God's goal is attained in that person.

"Proclamation has as its goal the bringing of people to this knowledge and trust. How radically this faith involves our whole life is shown by the New Testament's equation of faith with obedience. So it is clear that, because of the nature of faith, no tension can exist between "Christ alone" and the "addition" of faith. Faith lives solely from Christ, and is filled by what he has done ... Christ's attainment of the goal for us (but without us) and his attainment of the goal in us are not concurrent.

"Yet it is this very emptiness of faith in itself which leads to its decisive character. Because it is directed solely to Christ and his work for us, faith is necessary-and its lack excludes one from salvation. Without faith, God's goal in us is not reached. Precisely because faith is neither a human accomplishment nor a human contribution, but rather a confession that everything has been done for us by Christ, we have no Christ if we have no faith. This is why Scripture speaks so strongly about the necessity, value, and power of faith. Faith receives value only from its object. And because of faith's necessity, we are bound to speak of the mortal peril of unbelief."[4]

Humility is the characteristic of believing that gives us the ability to admit our needs, weaknesses, and limitations so that we can submit to the power of God in our life and receive our strength from Him and through others. It is not powerlessness. It knows where the power comes from. Humility is the beginning of faith that love works in us as we look outside of ourselves to I AM. Humility involves being able to give to others but also to receive from others as we keep our eyes fixed on I AM and thereby become more like Him in love. The key characteristic of humility is mercifulness. The loss of humility brings about rebelliousness.

Belief is an overwhelming sense of hope based on understanding of past actions and in the fulfillment of future promises that gives encouragement so that we can be enthusiastic and self-stretching, in order that we might grow through developing (God-given) potential. The key characteristic of belief is hopefulness. The loss of belief brings about despair.

Trust is the characteristic outgrowth of believing that gives us the ability to be open and share who we are and what we have been given so that we can be catalysts in the development of openness and candor in others. The key characteristic of trust is openness. The loss of trust brings about suspiciousness.

Acceptance is the characteristic outgrowth of believing that gives us the ability to forgive ourselves and others so that healing and understanding can take place. The key characteristic of acceptance is forgiveness. The loss of acceptance brings about a judgmental nature.

Confidence is the characteristic outgrowth of believing that gives us assurance of our being accepted and gives us the ability to look past self-promotion to the promotion of others so that their confidence is built up. The key characteristic of confidence is assuredness or certainty. The loss of confidence brings about inconsistency.

Gratitude is the characteristic outgrowth of believing that gives us the ability to look at all good things as gifts from God and causes us to give in return so the gifts can be shared by all. The key characteristic of gratitude is thankfulness. The loss of gratitude brings about an expecting nature—ungratefulness.

Compassion is the characteristic outgrowth of believing that gives us the ability to be gracious (giving undeserved favor) and merciful (not demanding retribution) so that we might live in a way that will be most beneficial to ourselves and others and glorifying to God. The key characteristic of compassion is graciousness. The loss of compassion brings about degradation, using of others.

Freedom is the characteristic outgrowth of believing that gives us the ability to set aside personal desires and postpone pleasure (i.e., physical and emotional gratification) in order that we are liberated to find complete satisfaction in God and be separated from enslaving entanglements. The key characteristic of freedom is purposefulness. The loss of freedom brings about insatiability, inability to be satisfied.

Stewardship is the characteristic of believing that gives us the ability to be interconnected with each other in a truly loving manner. We do not lose any integral parts of ourselves or disintegrate into another person, yet we value and need each other's gifts and uniqueness for the full use and completion of our own giftedness. The key characteristic of stewardship is carefulness. The loss of stewardship brings about codependence, an inability to be helpful.

Servanthood is the characteristic of believing that gives us the ability to worship in everything that we do by looking to God to fill us and overflow through us into the lives of others for thoughtful attentiveness to God's desires for them. The key characteristic of servanthood is submissiveness or interdependence. The loss of servanthood brings about an uncaring attitude, inattentiveness.

Loyalty is the characteristic outgrowth of believing that gives us the ability to remain true or faithful to I AM, ourselves, and others so that we are not pushed or led along by demands other than God's. The key characteristic of loyalty is faithfulness. The loss of loyalty brings about inconsistency.

Purity is the characteristic outgrowth of believing that gives us the ability to be unmixed in our allegiance toward God so that we won't be driven by any other purpose than to love, glorify, and enjoy God to the ultimate benefit, enjoyment, and fulfillment of ourselves and others. The key characteristic of purity is objectiveness (integrity, congruence). The loss of purity brings about confusion.

Justice is the characteristic outgrowth of believing that gives us the ability to act rightly on behalf of God so that despots (those who want to control, oppress, and use others for personal gain) are not allowed to triumph and the defenseless are defended. The key characteristic of justice is righteousness. The loss of justice brings about either apathy or being overbearing (despotism).

Rest is the characteristic of believing that gives us the ability see past obstacles to our own well-being and the well-being of others so that we can peacefully work to overcome those obstacles and overthrow those who are setting them up. The key characteristic of rest is peacefulness. The loss of rest brings about anxiety, panic.

Determination is the characteristic of believing that gives us the ability to persist until that which has been started is completed. The key characteristic of determination is steadfastness, completion. The loss of determination brings about an inability to follow through, indecision.

2 Corinthians 13:5: "Examine yourselves, to see whether you are in the faith. Test yourselves. Or do you not realize this about yourselves, that Jesus Christ is in you?—unless indeed you fail to meet the test!"

We are meant for a kingdom much better than Camelot or any kingdom we can imagine on this earth. Anthony Hoekema writes, "The Kingdom of God, therefore, is to be understood as the reign of God dynamically active in human history through Jesus Christ, the purpose of which is the redemption of God's people from sin and from demonic powers, and the final establishment of the new heavens and the new earth. It means the great drama of the history of salvation has been inaugurated, and that the new age has been ushered in. The Kingdom must not be understood as merely the salvation of certain individuals or even as the reign of God in the hearts of his people; it means nothing less than the reign of God over his entire created universe ...

"It will be evident, therefore, that the kingdom of God, as described in the New Testament, is not a state of affairs brought about by human achievement, nor is it the culmination of strenuous human effort. The kingdom is established by God's sovereign grace, and its blessings are to be received as gifts of that grace. Man's duty is not to bring the kingdom into existence, but to enter into it by faith, and to pray that he may be enabled more and more to submit himself to the beneficent rule of God in every area of his life. The kingdom is not man's upward climb to perfection but God's breaking into human history to establish his reign and to advance his purposes.

"It should be added that the kingdom of God includes both positive and a negative aspect. It means redemption for those who accept it and enter into it by faith, but judgment for those who reject it."[5]

Absolute love never fails. I AM, the three in one, will bring about a world of love for all who have had faith in Him throughout human history. When all whom He has established as His are complete, we will eternally live in His presence without a wandering heart. Matthew

24:13–14: "But the one who endures to the end will be saved. And this gospel of the kingdom will be proclaimed throughout the whole world as a testimony to all nations, and then the end will come."

Enduring to the end and proclaiming the kingdom of God primarily are done through living a life that is connected to I AM.

> 2 Peter 1:2–8: May grace and peace be multiplied to you in the knowledge of God and of Jesus our Lord. His divine power has granted to us all things that pertain to life and godliness, through the knowledge of him who called us to his own glory and excellence, by which he has granted to us his precious and very great promises, so that through them you may become partakers of the divine nature, having escaped from the corruption that is in the world because of sinful desire. For this very reason, make every effort to supplement your faith with virtue, and virtue with knowledge, and knowledge with self-control, and self-control with steadfastness, and steadfastness with godliness, and godliness with brotherly affection, and brotherly affection with love. For if these qualities are yours and are increasing, they keep you from being ineffective or unfruitful in the knowledge of our Lord Jesus Christ.

As we rest in determination waiting for the beginning, the continual looking away from self to I AM, to absolute love, will be the way home.

This beginning is experienced by most of us through death. The journey begins through humility, but we also wait for completion of the race. Revelation 22:17: "The Spirit and the Bride say, 'Come.' And let the one who hears say, 'Come.' And let the one who is thirsty come; let the one who desires take the water of life without price."

Revelation 22:20: "He who testifies to these things says, 'Surely I am coming soon.' Amen. Come, Lord Jesus!"

End Notes

1. Gilbert, Daniel. *Stumbling on Happiness.* Vintage Books, New York, NY, 2006, page 4.
2. Piper, Dr. John. *Future Grace.* Multnomah Books, Sisters, OR, 1995, page 243.
3. Wells, David F. *Above All Earthly Pow'rs: Christ in a Post Modern World.* Wm. B. Eerdmans Publishing, Grand Rapids, MI, 2005, page 206.
4. Koenig, Adrio. *The Eclipse of Christ in Eschatology: Toward a Christ Centered Approach.* Wm. B. Eerdmans Publishing, Grand Rapids, MI, 1989, pages 158 and 159., M. I., Marshall, Morgan and Scott, London, England, Adapted from Jesus die Laast, Gelowig Nagedink Deel 2, Praetoria, DRC Bookshop, 1980.
5. Hoekema, Anthony A. *The Bible and the Future.* Wm. B. Eerdmans Publishing, Grand Rapids, MI, 1979, page 45.

Afterword

This book *is not intended to be an ending* but a beginning. Genesis starts out, "In the beginning, God ..." and this is precisely the point of this book. God is knowable, yet our knowing of God is inexhaustible. Where God is, there is life and growth. God is life, God is love, God is truth, and God is light. "In Him there is no darkness." 1 John 1:5

If this book has given you a desire to learn more about *absolute love*, I do not know of anyone who has done more to show the connection between our good and the absolute glory of God than John Piper. You can discover more at www.desiringgod.org. Some other very good resources are www.sovereigngraceministries.org and www.enjoyinggodministries.org.

For Muslims who want to find more information on Isa Al-Masih, or the Injeel of Isa, more information can be found at www.crescentproject.org.

If you are Jewish, you can find out more about Yeshua of Nazareth www.jewsforjesus.org.

For scientists who are seeking some reference with other scientists who are not closed to researching and are open to the possibility that the intricate wonders of the world are from an absolute source and not random, refer to places like www.whomadegod.org, www.worldbydesign.org, and www.icr.org.

If you want to help with various types of rescue ministries, to give sacrificial love to help people who are in some type of lie or bondage you could contact some of the following organizations.

www.worldvision.org

www.humantrafficking.org

www.amnestyusa.org

www.unicef.org

www.nrlc.org

www.harborhouse.org

www.lifesaverministries.org

www.prisonfellowship.org

www.exodusinternational.org

www.compassion.com

"Whatever is true, whatever is honorable, whatever is just, whatever is pure, whatever is lovely, whatever is commendable, if there is any excellence, if there is anything worthy of praise, think about these things." Philippians 4:8.

Sola Scriptura, Sola Fide, Sola Gratia, Solo Christos, Soli Deo Gloria

O.T. Hesed Exodus 34:6,7 "ABSOLUTE LOVE N.T. Agape 1 John 4:8:16

CHARACTER OF GOD(The Sovereign, Personal, Self-Revealing ,Self-Existent, Relational God)YHWH-Yeshua, Jesus, 'Isa

Applying Truth 1 Cor. 13:7;Gal. 5:6	Motivation-Faith Working Through Love		Relational Affect	Suppressing Truth 2 Cor. 2:14-16;Heb. 10:26-31;1 John 4:18
	Qualities of Faith	Character Qualities		Motivation-Fear/Shame
	Spiritual	Psychological	Sociological/Physiological	Antipathy/Fear — Physical/Material
	Humility	Mercifulness	Ability to be vulnerable/receive from others	Rebelliousness/Full of Self
	Belief	Hopefulness	Ability to be encouraging	Despairing/Lost
	Trust	Openness	Ability to share/be transparent	Stinginess/Suspicious
	Acceptance	Forgiveness	Ability to absorb pain/facilitate healing	Judgmental/Self-destructive
	Confidence	Assuredness	Ability to know and accept self	Uncertainty/Inconsistency
	Gratitude	Thankfulness	Ability to see life as a gift/be giving in order to receive something greater.	Ungrateful/Expecting
	Compassion	Graciousness	Ability to go beyond what is deserved	Using/Degrading
	Freedom	Purposefulness	Ability to postpone/forego temporal unfulfilling wants	Insatiable/Controlled by desires
	Stewardship	Carefulness	Ability to be beneficial of others	Codependent/Unhelpful
	Servanthood	Submissiveness-Interdependence	Ability to attend to the needs of others	Inattentive/Uncaring/Needy
	Loyalty	Faithfulness –Being True	Ability to stand consistently beside others	Unreliable/Inconsistent
	Purity	Objectiveness,	Ability to be certain/unmixed/integral	Incongruent/Confused
	Justice	Righteousness	Ability to stand against oppression	Bullying/Overbearing/Apathetic
	Determination	Steadfastness	Ability to continue until the end	Indecisive/Cannot follow through
	Rest	Peacefulness	Ability to look beyond obstacles to a greater reward beyond, not inactivity;	Anxiety/Panic
	Results in the "Obedience of Faith"	Christ likeness		Results in Lawlessness, Perversion Apathy / Pathology / Inability
	Rom. 1:5,16:26;James 1:25		Ability to be Truly-Loving-Caring/LOVE is active.	Rom.1:18:32;Rom. 8:7&8; 1 Tim. 1:8-11;1 John 3:4
			Counterfeit/ Perverted	
			Relativism(humanistic orientation) or self-righteousness(religious orientation)	

Faith is a supernatural phenomenon developed and experienced through God, by the empowerment of the Holy Spirit, working through WORD of God, to build up the Body of Christ! John 13:34,35; Acts 2:41-47; Eph.4:4-16; 1 John 5:2-5 (Proclamation, Worship, Fellowship, Mission)